DD376455

VALIDATION
IS FOR PARKING

VALIDATION
IS FOR PARKING

*How Women Can Beat
the Confidence Con*

NICOLE KALIL

LIONCREST
PUBLISHING

Validation Is for Parking

How Women Can Beat the Confidence Con

ISBN 978-1-5445-3268-4 Hardcover
      978-1-5445-3269-1 Paperback
      978-1-5445-3270-7 Ebook

For Jalyn.
The answer to the question will always be,
"All the time."
Every second of every day.
No matter what.

And for my Mom.
Because the answer was always
the same for me, too.

Contents

PART 3: FIVE CONFIDENCE DERAILERS AND THEIR ANTIDOTES, THE CONFIDENCE BUILDERS

Introduction

You've been conned.

That was the thought repeating in my head after a coworker told me, "I wish I had your confidence." I had just received a massive promotion I'd been working on getting for years. We were celebrating in our conference room with the rest of our team, and all I could think was, *You've been conned. You all have...by me.*

I was to become the first woman to take the role of Chief Development Officer at the Fortune 100 company where I worked. I'd been hustling my ass off[1] to make a name for myself, stockpiling titles and accolades in the heavily male-dominated finance industry. By all accounts, I was killing it, looking the part of a trailblazing woman set on world domination and attracting attention in the process. Other women looked up to me, wondering how they, too, could smash the glass ceiling. It wasn't the first time I'd gotten a compliment similar to the one my coworker gave me that day, but every time anyone commented on my confidence or success, I'd

---

[1] The playlist of my life at the time: Workin' Day and Night, She Works Hard For The Money, Takin' Care Of Business, Work Bitch... You get the idea.

cringe inside. It would send me into a tailspin no one else would ever see. I'd smile and say thank you (because the role of "successful woman" came with a list of dos and don'ts, and smiling was a definite must-do) but what I really wanted to scream was, "I wish I had the confidence you *think* I have!"

I was a fraud living in constant fear of being found out. The image I presented to the world wasn't even close to an accurate representation of who I was. Let's just say I was living the longest distance in space and time away from my truth. I had become an Oscar-worthy actor in the role of my life and, like so many women, I'd wholeheartedly embraced faking it. In addition to conquering the business world, I was single and seemingly loving it. After all, who had time for a husband and kids when there was money to be made and ladders to climb? I had bought my first house long before most of my peers could afford to, and my desire to prove myself fueled me. *Yes, I'm successful; and yes, I want everyone to know it.*

But how it seemed wasn't how it was. I was caught in a loop of feeling like shit and doing whatever I could to make it look good. Loneliness, self-loathing, and doubt were my constant companions. The only place where I felt remotely capable was at work, but I questioned myself constantly in every aspect of my life. My inner monologue had beat-up mode on repeat, and no achievement was ever enough. When I got promoted, I immediately started questioning my ability to do the job, and once I started getting good at it, I set my sights on a higher position. When I got a raise, all I could think after the initial excitement and subsequent spending spree wore off was, "That's nice, but it's not enough." I was earning a more-than-decent income but still struggling to make ends meet because I had a more-than-decent spending problem.

Work was the *good* part of my life, even with the constant struggles of navigating the boys' club. In my personal life, I'd wasted *years* staying committed to a guy I was no longer in a relationship with. Because he would never love me back, I believed I was fundamentally unlovable. I genuinely thought if I just looked skinny enough, said and did the right things, and could prove myself worthy, he'd finally see what he'd been missing and change into the man he'd never actually been—but that I thought he *could* be.[2] I was both too much and never enough. I had tied all my value to my physical appearance, status, and income. I was indeed a con artist, but the con was on me. I secretly lived in fear of someone finding out the truth about my "confidence." It was all for show. It was an act I put on for everyone else, and it was slowly killing me.

Keeping up appearances had become a second full-time job that had me running ragged. I knew it was just a matter of time before I'd be exposed and all my faults and failures would be used against me. As a working woman, I had already experienced how my strengths were misinterpreted—people called me "reactive" when I thought

---

[2] Sadly, I repeated this pattern with a couple of oh-so-lucky men because I truly thought relationships were supposed to be hard, and proving myself was my general M.O.

I was being passionate, or "opinionated" when I spoke up—so I couldn't even begin to imagine what people would do and say if they saw my flaws. I was emotionally overworked, and the payment for my overtime was stress, anxiety, and exhaustion. To become the "perfect woman" I thought I needed to be, I multitasked my face off until I couldn't any longer. When I hit my version of rock bottom, which included equal parts alcohol and regret, my problem finally became clear to me. I didn't know what confidence was, but I was certain I didn't have it.

Like so many of us, I'd been fed a line of bullshit about what it means to be a confident woman. That was problematic in itself, but the real issue was that I had *bought into* the bullshit. I believed being confident came as a result of being perfect, so I was striving to make everything in my life *look* perfect in order to get there. My body became a metaphor for my life. I made myself small in all the places I was supposed to, but was also keenly aware of what needed to be accentuated and noticed. I highlighted, lifted, shaped, emphasized, hid, revealed, confined, squeezed, starved, and consumed in the unhealthiest ways possible. I emulated real and fictional people whose lives seemed aspirational in a desperate attempt to become them. Am I the only person who thought Samantha from *Sex and the City* was the spirit guide of how to be single and professionally driven? (Nothing wrong with Samantha, for the record, but my goal to carbon-copy her was inauthentic at best.) I thought if I could just be more like *this* male colleague or *that* famous singer, or meet *the* guy, I might finally be happy. And in striving to become someone else, I became utterly disconnected from myself.

A DESPERATELY NEEDED WAKE-UP CALL

While I never actually attempted suicide during this time of living my fake life, the thought of it would swirl through my mind. I began asking myself whether I mattered. Hypothetically, if I made the choice to end my life, how long would it take for someone outside of work to notice? Would people be shocked? How could I do that to my parents, sister, and friends who had no idea how horrible I felt and how wildly confused I'd become about who I was? The only option, in my mind, was to keep faking it. I'd keep showing up to work and pretending to be one of the guys like I always had so people would think I was bold, stoic, and fearless. But somewhere deep down, I also knew I had to make a change before my lifestyle destroyed me.

My first turning point came in the form of a transformational learning course I'd signed up for to please a boyfriend and disguised as professional development. The work held a mirror up in front of my face and forced me to take a good, hard look at myself—the eating disorder, the workaholism, the binge drinking, the depression, the reckless dating habits. It was all there tearing me apart regardless of how "Independent Woman" my life seemed from the outside. I didn't like myself. Even worse, I didn't *trust* myself, and the moment had come to get brutally honest about it.

Around this time, I started working to bring more women into my industry by offering advice and mentoring within my company. Previously, I'd avoided "women's events" like the plague. I just wanted to be a great leader, not a great *female* leader. So nobody was more surprised than I when I discovered that doing this sort of work provided me an initial "why" to focus on, since doing something for myself wasn't a good enough reason for me yet. I was passionate and engaged for the first time in a long time and could see how I could make a difference that mattered beyond a result or a goal achieved. I began to recognize that other women were dealing with a lot of the same issues I was, and a small light suddenly cut through my darkness. My confusion about confidence wasn't just a me-problem. Countless other women were struggling like I was, trying to stuff themselves into boxes made of masculine expectations that didn't actually fit their desires, truths, or personalities and never would. When it became clear that I wasn't totally alone, hopelessly flawed, or a broken woman, I got serious about being the confident person everyone thought I was, but I had no idea where to start. In the steady stream of experts that yell from the mountaintops, "BE CONFIDENT!" I had yet to find someone in the know who would take me aside and tell me *how* to actually do it.

As is true for so many people, my pain became the catalyst toward the first steps of a journey that would ultimately change my entire life. I became a student of confidence, burning through every book and article on the subject that I could get my hands on. I began to observe and realize that many of the people I'd admired as confident were actually something else entirely. I had put my authenticity on the back burner so I could live their truth, but most of them were also performing to mask their insecurities. They didn't have the answers I needed. No one did. If I was going to build a life I loved, I was going to have to get vulnerable and start trusting *myself*. To do that, I had to move toward my truth. The time had come to take off my own mask and keep it off for good.

I was terrified.

There I was in my early thirties, with very little idea of who I actually was, recovering from what seemed like my 218th heartbreak, living in a house I couldn't afford, and counting the minutes during the weekends until I could get back to work. I was committed to applying what I'd learned in the transformational learning course I'd taken and testing out the things I was learning about confidence in very small ways. There were a million tiny action steps I was taking, which led me to one of the biggest, scariest opportunities for me at the time: I met a guy.

I know that doesn't seem so scary, but to say it was freaking me out would be a gross understatement. Now, I want to be clear: this isn't a story of how meeting the man I eventually married gave me confidence. That's not what happened at all. What did happen was, because I'd been focused on my confidence, I showed up completely differently with this guy than I ever had with any of the others. I was wildly imperfect. I trusted myself to take things slowly rather than putting pressure on him and myself to know where our connection was headed. It wasn't until six months after we met that we went out on our first date. I asked questions. I told him what was important to me. I shared my fears. I was *real,* and it was the scariest thing I'd ever done. So many times, I was convinced I'd blown it, but I kept putting myself out there. Yes, I ended up marrying him, but I know for sure that if I'd met him just a year earlier, I wouldn't have even noticed him. Likewise, he definitely wouldn't have been impressed with me.

A couple of years after meeting and dating my now-husband Jay, I made another risky decision, which was to cut the cord and quit my lucrative job. I was having the greatest impact and finding the most joy in mentoring women in my industry, but I knew that my role would never allow me to turn that passion into my primary focus. The career I'd worked so hard to build had become a distraction from what I really wanted to be doing. The titles and promotions no longer mattered. I was tired of proving myself, and I finally acknowledged I wasn't ever going to get what I felt I deserved from my current company. My mission to build up other women while I was creating confidence in myself was huge and complex, and I needed to make space for it. I felt clearer about my purpose; and although fear and doubt gripped me, I wasn't going to let them stand in my way any longer. It was time to start my own business where I could show up as my best self, even if that meant risking it all and putting my imperfections on display.

My managing partner supported my decision to leave. (Thank God for allies!) We helped each other with a transition plan, so he wasn't left high and dry, and I wasn't immediately jumping into the deep end of the pool. Six months later, I made my move and went from being a consistent breadwinner to bringing home exactly zero bacon. Our household income shrank considerably, and while I acknowledge my privilege in knowing Jay and I weren't going to end up homeless, the shift wasn't an easy pill to swallow. I made mistakes and pivoted many times but also had some big wins. By the second birthday of my female-focused coaching and consulting business, I'd matched the CDO salary I'd previously been making. By the third year, I'd doubled it. By the fourth, I felt like I was "killing it" all over again. So what did I do? Well, the time had come to take another leap of faith. I was still in my comfort zone, working in the finance industry. Spending all my time in that space was keeping doors shut that I wanted to throw wide open; so in 2019, I walked away from my two biggest contracts, which totaled over half a million dollars in revenue.

Today, my business doesn't revolve around finance or any specific industry. My business isn't even about business. It's about something so much bigger. The opportunity to coach many, many women and leaders led me to the work we'll cover in this book. Confidence is the bridge to better relationships, more success, and loving the life you live. Women's lack of confidence is apparent in the business world, but this issue touches more than our careers. It's a problem that ripples out into every corner of our lives, contributing to everything we are, think, have, and do. It doesn't have to be this way. Our confidence didn't go anywhere! It never left us, it's not lost, and no one and nothing else is holding onto it for us. I believe it's always there inside us, available any time we want to access it. So the question isn't, "Do you have confidence?" It's, "Are you connected to your confidence?" When you are, you can use it to design your life in whatever way you choose. The sky's the limit—glass ceiling be damned.

RECOVERY FROM VALIDATION ADDICTION

Logically, I know (now) that perfection is an impossible standard. I get (now) that it's a cruel game nobody ever wins. But I played anyway and lost myself in the process. My guess is that most of you reading this are also trying to be perfect but still feeling "less- than" and wondering what authentically confident people have that you don't. You might feel confident in certain areas of your life but still suffer from crippling fear or doubt in others. You might also have an inaccurate view of confidence in your mind, making you feel like you have to "fake it 'til you make it." When we're unclear about what confidence is and the inner effort it takes to build it, we can end up working insanely hard without getting any closer to real confidence, like a hamster stuck on a wheel. If that is where you are, I see you and am glad you're here. You're not alone, it's not your fault, and I'm here to give you tools to bridge the gap.

Here's the first thing you need to know: the message you're constantly being bombarded with is ass-backward. Everywhere you look, you're told that if you do this, buy that, or get to some point other than where you are, *then* you'll feel confident. I call this idea the "false equation," and it's the basis of the entire confidence con. What we've all been told over and over is that "If X happens, then I'll feel confident." X can be a million different things—a specific weight or size, a certain level of income, attention from the right person, a compliment, marrying the person of your dreams, a well-decorated home, perfectly behaved kids, big boobs, flawless skin... The list is endless, and it doesn't matter which X you choose, because the formula won't work. This equation tells you that in order to be confident, you must first *do* something, and then someone or something needs to come along and validate it. It's complete and utter bullshit, but we've been conned for so long that we operate from this false equation on the regular.

Well, if the false equation doesn't work, then what does? Here's the answer: "When I'm confident, I have a higher probability of X." What's great about this new equation is that even if X doesn't happen, you can still be confident! It's not a chicken-or-egg question, because what comes first is clear. When you're confident, you'll have a higher probability of attracting and choosing your dream partner because you'll show up as *yourself* when you're with them. When you're confident, you're more likely to raise your hand, advocate for yourself, and bring your unique talents and gifts to your career, so you're more likely to get the promotion. When you're confident, you're more likely to take the risks necessary for achieving the success that will allow you to buy the fancy car or go on the expensive vacation. This is all obvious and logical when we think about it, but it goes directly against the lies we've internalized.

As a woman, you have every right to be confused about confidence. You've been conned. We all have. Religion, culture, business, the media, advertising, entertainment, our education system, and other influences have sent the message in every possible way of how to be a "good" woman and how easy it is to be a "bad" one. Who I am, and who *you* are, as a woman has likely been defined by everyone but us. Women have not historically been the deciders, but many of us have been recruited as enforcers. Let's look at work as an example. For a long time, it was socially unacceptable for a married woman to work, and it was expected for women to get married young; so the structures and expectations of work cultures were designed for and by men. Times have changed, however, and although women now make up over half the labor force, companies are still disproportionately led by men. A whopping 92 percent of business books are written by men in modern-day society. Most of what we learn about being in business, we learn from men. Yet women are still expected to dive head-first into professional systems and strategies created, defined, and reinforced by men and somehow thrive. Maybe the struggle to do so doesn't align with your personal experience. If that's the case, I'm thrilled for you! But I could fill this book with examples of all the ways I was told to show up in this world, regardless of whether or not it aligned with who I am.

Since starting my own business, I've had the privilege of connecting with thousands of women of all ages from all over the country. I can say with clarity that perfectionism is a plague that has infected every one of us. We're trying to do it all, have it all, be it all, and look good in the process, while wearing ourselves out trying to make it look effortless. Here's the rub, though: Feeling the need to perform and be perfect forces us to give away our power to whomever or whatever we're performing for. Like junkies seeking our next fix, we find ourselves on a perpetual hunt for fresh validation. We *need* that next compliment, promotion, achievement, relationship, or result in order to feel worthy. We need something or someone outside of ourselves to tell us we're okay in order for us to believe it. The opportunity we all have, and what I'm encouraging you to consider, is to separate our confidence from any external source and reclaim trust in ourselves. Confidence is an inside job. Real, unshakeable trust is not about what anything *looks* like. It's about what it *is*.

This journey probably won't be elegant, easy, or straightforward like we're led to believe by the army of seemingly flawless experts, motivational speakers, and influencers on social media. In my experience, it's raw, messy work that requires tons of trial and error.

The way women build confidence is nuanced and, in many ways, different from how others do it because the ways we're socialized and the challenges we face are different. This is especially true in business. For instance, we often define leadership in masculine terms, and so when a man demonstrates traditionally masculine qualities like decisiveness, strategic thinking, assertiveness, power, and influence, he's seen as a leader. A woman demonstrating the same qualities, though, is often considered too aggressive or to be a bitch.[3] Now, don't get me wrong—I'm not saying men are bad leaders. I've read hundreds of books written by men and can attest to their incredible insights, valuable lessons, and great tips. But those men lack an understanding of the female experience and, I'm guessing, in most cases, unconsciously emphasize the masculine while ignoring the feminine. We need a working definition of confidence that goes beyond gender and won't fall apart under scrutiny, both in business and in life.

THE ROAD TO TRUSTING OURSELVES AGAIN

Ultimately, this is a love story wrapped in a business book (with a decent amount of cursing, to boot). I'm not talking about the love we have for others, but the love we must have for ourselves. This book is the guide to building confidence that I wish I'd had. We're

---

[3] I know this one from experience.

going to talk about real confidence, why women struggle to build it, the circumstances that chip away at it, and actionable steps *you* can take to beat the confidence con.

My lack of confidence used to stand between me and myself, as well as between me and everything I'd always wanted. But I realized over time that anyone can build the skill of confidence with enough desire, knowledge, and the work of getting into action. The benefits of building my confidence were priceless for me. I'm now a joyfully married entrepreneur and mother to an incredibly loved daughter, living my purpose and my truth, and working to help other women become their best selves. No more starving myself or drowning in self-hatred. Please don't interpret this as a claim that my life is perfect and I have it all figured out. It isn't, and I don't. I'm not sure that building your confidence will bring you a marriage, family, career, or happiness (if those are things you're going for). At the same time, I can't think of a single scenario or opportunity where trusting yourself wouldn't make life better, fuller, and richer. What I can say at this point is that I truly like myself the way I am, and I want you to, as well. My happiness is finally in my own hands; and if I can do it, so can you. I don't consider myself the ultimate authority on matters of confidence, but I have created an effective system of confidence-building tactics that caters to the female experience.

I wrote this book with women in mind, but I don't advocate for us at the expense of men, and I sincerely hope anyone of any gender will find great value in reading it. Additionally, I acknowledge that I do not speak for or represent all women. I'm an able-bodied, straight, agnostic, white-passing woman with socioeconomic privilege. My intention was to be inclusive and thoughtful in my language and examples while writing this book, but I'll probably have missed the mark at times. I hope you can look past any failings on my part to the greater message of trusting yourself and living with confidence. In the end, that's what matters most.

This work is never done, so it's important to know that I'm still making my way through the journey right along with you. Imagine having the courage to keep moving toward what matters, even if everything in your life seems to be veering off-course, because you know you're meant to. Imagine knowing you'll be fine, or maybe even come out *better* than before, when you fail or someone doesn't like you. Imagine living in the belief that the universe is rigged in your favor and that everything will ultimately be for the best. This is not about creating the perfect life where you never have to struggle, feel unsure about what to do, or face any fears. That doesn't exist. Instead, it's about being able to trust yourself throughout every experience life throws at you—the good, the bad, and everything in between. There are countless paths we can take to change our lives for the better. No matter what, building your confidence is always a choice that bears fruit. I'm inviting you to begin, to build, to grow…because wherever your current level of confidence may be, there's always an opportunity to have more of it.

If you're open to the concept that we've become disconnected from what confidence actually is, it's logical to first get clear on the true definition of confidence and why it matters. Let's dive in (or cannonball, toe-touch, belly-flop . . . whatever mode of getting into the water works for you)!

PART 1

CONFIDENCE AND THE FEMALE EXPERIENCE

CHAPTER 1

What Confidence Is, What It Isn't, and Why It Matters

*"To be yourself in a world that is
constantly trying to make you something else
is the greatest accomplishment."*

—RALPH WALDO EMERSON

AS YOU CAN IMAGINE, I spend a lot of time talking with people —especially women—about confidence. One thing that's become obvious is that the word "confidence" is constantly being used when we mean something else. It has become a catch-all word we throw around without even realizing we're doing it. I used to confuse confidence with perfection, as I explained earlier. Recently, a woman I was coaching used it as a precursor to motivation. "If I was more confident, I'd feel more like doing what I'm supposed to be doing." That doesn't quite fit, either. You can be motivated and not confident, motivated and confident, or even unmotivated and confident. They're separate things that can intersect or work alongside each other, but they're not identical. Courage, for another example, is often equated with confidence, and while one might lead to the other, they work in different ways. Even in the context of all the work I do about what derails confidence and how to build it, I *still* catch myself using the word incorrectly. The language we use matters. It informs how we think about our reality and our place within it, so having an ass-backward definition of something as important as confidence is not only confusing, but also massively problematic.

We, as a global society, don't understand what confidence is. Our lack of understanding isn't because we're dumb. It's because we've been lied to and grown accustomed to the word being misused. When it comes to the female experience, this misuse is particularly debilitating because we're expected to show up confidently in so many aspects of our lives, but we're getting mixed messages about how to do so. We're surrounded by examples of confidence that are anything but, and we're often told that being confident requires us to show up as someone we're not. Good, bad, or indifferent, men have been the deciders of so many of the environments we live and work in. When we, as women, try to fit ourselves into boxes built by systems and structures (patriarchy, I'm looking at you) that were created without our input and weren't designed with us in mind, we become confused about what confidence is and feel separated from our authentic selves. The same is also true for men who feel they need to act a certain way to be perceived as confident. The bottom line is that our collective confusion about confidence hurts us all, though probably not equally.

We need a new definition of confidence that serves every one of us and remains accurate across the board—one that doesn't fall to tatters under scrutiny. In this chapter, I'm going to provide that definition so you can get clear on what true confidence is, what it isn't, and why the distinction matters.

DEFINING CONFIDENCE

At its core, confidence is all about *trust*. The word itself evolved from the Latin noun *confidentia*, which meant "full trust" (con- or "with" + fīdō, or "trust") when it was borrowed by Middle English in the late sixteenth century. The definition was expanded in our language to include "the feeling or belief that one can rely on someone or something" or "a feeling of self-assurance arising from one's appreciation of one's own abilities or qualities." In most other languages, the word *confidence* translates to or is defined by the word *trust* (although *faith* and *belief* come up a lot, too). I won't bore you with a slew of dictionary info, but the etymology of the word is important. We have to frame confidence in a way that's true to the word's origin and provides clarity in terms of how we see ourselves and others. So, what's a functional definition that gives more insight into how we can build self-trust?

Here's the definition of confidence I operate from and will be using for the purposes of this book:

> *Confidence is knowing who you are,*
> *owning who you're not,*
> *and choosing to embrace all of it.*

If that still feels too complicated, you can think of it in even simpler terms: Confidence is trusting yourself, firmly and boldly.

We'll use this as our working definition of confidence, but also as a litmus test for the misinterpreted and misused examples of confidence we've been given by society. Let's take physical appearance as an example. You can hardly go on any social media platform, see any advertisement, or follow just about any influencer without running into some version of "If you buy this product, fit into this size, have this shape, lift this, sculpt that, eliminate those wrinkles, dress like this (but not like that), wear this designer label"... You get the idea. "You'll be more confident!" This is one of the most pervasive examples of the word *confidence* being used when we mean something else entirely. Why? Because the people who want to sell you stuff *know* you want to be confident. If someone could tell me how the actual fuck buying red-bottomed shoes or getting botox would help me trust myself more, I might reevaluate. I've bought the labels, dressed the part, been a size four with a C-cup bra, and *none* of those things has built trust in myself. In fact, in some cases, those kinds of choices can actually erode your confidence if you're making them to fill a void, or because you ultimately feel bad about yourself and think they'll fix it. What fits better here is to say, "If you buy this, do that, have this, and so on" you'll feel more *attractive* (or many other possible words, like *desirable, happy,* or *successful*). And there's nothing wrong with wanting to be any of those things! But call it what it is.

If confidence is about trust, then it begs the question of how we build trust in ourselves. We'll dig into all sorts of tactics later on, but the act of trusting ourselves hinges on knowing and embracing who we are. Part of trusting involves also knowing on a deep level who and what we're not, and embracing that, too. To know who we are and who we're not requires profound awareness of, and connection to, our authentic selves. What resonates with *you*? What makes *you* tick? What are *your* values and beliefs? How do *you* perceive and define *your* identity? What's *your* purpose in life? What's *your* value? Who do *you* want to be in a relationship with? Who or what should *you* walk toward, or away from? All of these kinds of questions come into play here, and the answers belong only to you.

I'll refer to my definition a lot over the course of this book, but I'll also encourage you to use trust as your litmus test. Does altering or improving your physical appearance make you trust yourself more? If so, it's a confidence builder. If not, it's something else (which doesn't necessarily make it a bad thing). Do your relationships support you in trusting yourself more? No other person can give you confidence, but they can definitely support you in fostering it. Or, is there a relationship you're in that has you trusting yourself less? If so, continuing in that relationship will erode your confidence and ultimately be unhealthy. I'm no expert on love; but too many women are in romantic relationships that do more damage to their trust in themselves than build it. Not trusting someone you love is painful and heartbreaking, but not trusting *yourself* is far worse. You can't break up with or separate from the person in the mirror.

As you can see, how the definition of confidence plays out is very personal in nature and will be different for everyone. I don't know the details of your authentic self. I don't know who you are, what you're not, or exactly what it will take for you to embrace that. You living in your confidence may present very differently from me living in mine. I'm not the decider of anyone else's choices about who or how they trust. I do know that understanding the real definition of confidence changed the game for me. I had to make the conscious decision to stop defining myself on everyone else's terms and start viewing my relationship with myself as both a priority and an ongoing journey. Not showing up authentically and honoring who I was turned me into a rabid validation junkie.[4] It led me to create the same

---

[4] Imagine this being said in a zombie movie. "VaLiDaaaaaaTiOn…"

problems for myself over and over until I hit rock bottom just like an addict. Know that as you make your way through this journey of coming home to yourself, you should not have to perform, hide, or cover up who you are. As you get further into shedding the false expectations of confidence we were all given, you'll also shed the desire or need to fake it. You get to be who you are and you get to trust yourself, no apologies necessary.

DEBUNKING CONFIDENCE

The most important thing to remember while doing this work is that confidence is not an outside-in proposition, but an inside-out one. This is why "validation-junkie" is the opposite of our goal. True confidence will never hinge on what other people think of you, because when that's your focus, you put all your personal power into their hands. That means it can be taken away from you at any time. Does that sound empowering? Of course not! Other people's opinions change more often than technology, and chasing after them will have you running in circles rather than feeling grounded, focused, and comfortable in your own skin. Throughout the course of my life, mainstream society's definition of a "confident woman" has changed so often I can no longer keep track. When I was young, magazines told me confidence looked like being thin, white, and blonde. Then it was about curves and big butts. (We can thank Sir Mix-A-Lot and Jennifer Lopez for that.) Then came

Beyoncé and her alter ego Sasha Fierce. I'm not cool enough to know who the image of confidence is now, but that person, too, will be replaced eventually. Who knows what the next picture-perfect version of a confident woman will be? Of course, you can look like Beyoncé *and* be confident (sign me up!) but one does not create the other.

If we're to beat the confidence con as women, we have to get past the obsessive focus on our appearance. A lot of us get confused about this, and rightly so. Let me be clear: the correlation between confidence and appearance is a complete racket no matter how much we try to make it true.

We often use the word *confidence* as a replacement for "feeling good." It's not the same, and the oversimplification is problematic because trusting yourself isn't contingent on feeling good. In fact, trusting yourself is far more useful when you're feeling bad. When you equate confidence with only good feelings, you'll end up thinking confidence is missing when you're experiencing "bad" feelings. Trusting yourself when everything is going well and you feel great is easy. Trusting yourself during tough times is when the real magic happens.

Confidence is also not about arrogance, competitiveness, condescension, ego, or being self-centered. That's a skewed, more masculine version of faux-confidence we've all been sold, especially in professional environments where we're often surrounded by examples of that energy. Both women and men try to live up to it for social approval, and it's problematic for all of us. Arrogance is created when you compare yourself to others and feel superior. It requires you to feel "better than" someone else, thereby making them "less than." Trusting yourself doesn't require you to rank yourself or others. Confidence is not needing to compare yourself to anyone at all.

We also often think that confidence is the same as extroversion. Just because someone has charisma or is high-energy, or has the gift of gab, being funny, or enjoying people does not mean they're confident. And just because someone feels uncomfortable in large groups, needs alone time, or isn't the life of the party doesn't mean they're less confident. Extroversion and introversion are about where you receive your energy from, and you can be confident or insecure either way.

As a side note, I've seen an uptick in instances of people saying things like, "This is just the way I am," and while that can sound like confidence, it misses the mark when it's used as a defense or an attack on someone else. The other day, one of my connections on social media posted a public service announcement declaring something to the effect of, "I'm not changing for anyone, even if my choices make things difficult for my friends and family! If you don't like it, fuck off!" This is not an example of confidence, but an over-rotation and a probable sign of underlying insecurities. Nobody thinks that way unless they're feeling afraid, attacked, or defensive. True confidence is quiet. Insecurities are loud.

UNDERSTANDING CONFIDENCE MATTERS

Confidence is crucial if we're to achieve success, however we choose to define that. In every sphere of personal development, whether it's related to our career, our love life, our family, our hobbies, or our friends, we're encouraged by a cacophony of coaches to "be more confident!" Its presence or lack thereof impacts every corner of our lives and can be a key differentiator in whether or not we discover and pursue our purpose. When I began repairing my trust with myself, I started making better decisions in every area of my life. Those decisions weren't always easier to make, but they became more obvious when I was connected to my truth. That change has impacted the dreams I've chased, the conversations I've had, the risks I've taken... It has permeated every aspect of my life!

Beyond the role confidence plays in our success, building true confidence just makes life simpler, and who couldn't use a little more of that? Bad things still happen in my life. I still face challenges. People still piss me off. I still get rejected. (Regularly!) There will always be mistakes, failures, fears, and doubts, but I'm able to move through those moments in much healthier ways than I used to. I don't internalize them and question everything about myself anymore. I'm not living in fear of being found out for being a fraud, and even more importantly, I no longer *am* a fraud. As far as I know, we only get one life and it belongs to us first and foremost. We may as well live it as truthfully and confidently as we can, because the alternative is stressful, emotionally exhausting, and confusing. Who can be happy living a lie? How can anyone live fully until they've embraced who they really are? It didn't work for me, even though it may have looked good from the outside.

Ask anyone to list the most important aspects of any healthy relationship and you'd be hard-pressed to find someone who didn't put trust in the top three. Fundamentally speaking, the most important relationship any of us will ever have is the one with ourselves. You can try to mentally and emotionally divorce yourself like I did in my twenties and early thirties, but you can't get physically separated. You can't throw all your clothes on the lawn and tell yourself to get out. You can't block yourself on Twitter. The only option for a fulfilling life is to love yourself unconditionally. As Oscar Wilde once wrote, "Be yourself; everyone else is already taken."

SEEING THE LIE

By now, you may be thinking about confidence differently, realizing it's not what you've been told. The silver lining is that it might be easier to develop than you think. Not *easy*, but *easier*. There's no scientific reason I can find that would have us believe women are born with less confidence than men. In fact, it would appear girls and boys have similar levels of confidence until the early years of elementary school. But generally speaking, we go through much of our lives, all the way until middle age, with less confidence than men. It's a complex issue and there's plenty of blame to go around in relation to the confidence con if we're looking to point fingers. We've been lied to . . . a lot. Many of us have bought into the lie and then held ourselves and others to its standards. To see the lie for what it is, we must take a look at how the confidence con plays out for women in everyday life.

CHAPTER 2

How the Confidence Con
Plays Out in Our Lives

"It's hard to be a woman.
You must think like a man, act like a lady,
look like a young girl, and
work like a horse."

—UNKNOWN

IN 2018, leadership development consultants Jack Zenger and Joseph Folkman published data that showed around 50 percent of men twenty-five or younger said they felt confident, while only 30 percent of women said the same. By their mid-forties, women and men rated themselves as equally confident. At age sixty, most women ended up surpassing men in confidence. After learning about this data, it's natural to ask why so many women lack confidence early in life. I get asked that question a lot and while I have my more polished answer at the ready, the real answer that always pops into my mind is…how the fuck could we *not*?

Think about how a girl grows up in our society. From the moment she's born, she's surrounded by the message that her value is in her ability to be cute, clean, quiet, respectful, helpful, and pleasing to others. The "boys will be boys" mantra allows little boys to get away with shit she never could, like roughhousing or rolling in the mud. "That's not nice, careful, or cute," she's told. (And don't get me started on how early "sexy" gets introduced. Don't believe me? Check out all the sexy Halloween costumes available for *eight-year-old girls.*) The media that surrounds her says "pretty" and "sexy" are of vital importance if you're a girl, which basically confirms and reinforces that she exists for the pleasure of others. She notices certain trends in the shows and movies she watches and, once she's old enough to get online, on social media too. Her appearance can't possibly measure up to the airbrushed and filtered photos of the "ideal woman" she's exposed to on a daily basis, so she begins to dislike her body and, by extension, herself as a whole. From an illegally young age, grown men leer, catcall, comment, and touch her without permission. She might be called an "underage woman," which is confusing because she's a *child*. Getting married and having kids is considered by others to be a foregone conclusion in her life, so she's introduced to caretaking chores early on. Many boys grow into adulthood without basic life skills like how to cook a chicken breast, wash the clothes they got dirty, or properly load a dishwasher.

(If you have a son and are teaching him these skills, give yourself a high five!) Tasks like these are upheld as priorities for her because of the assumption that she'll need to do them not only for herself, but for her family, too.

She's told if she's attractive and pleasing enough (because no other qualities matter as it relates to finding a man), someone great will choose her, and then she'll finally be complete.[5] And once married, she may continue to pursue her career, but has to work extra-hard to prove herself professionally while managing the lion's share of the household and caretaking responsibilities, which is another full-time job in itself.[6] At work, she questions herself constantly, worried that if she makes one mistake it'll be her professional demise. She feels pressure to hustle and grind, but is seen as difficult to work with if she speaks up too boldly in meetings or expresses disagreement with others. Self-doubt plagues her because the messages she receives don't resonate with how she feels. She doesn't feel comfortable taking risks or using her voice; she's often asked to take notes, so it's hard to speak up, anyway. She's told successful people are assertive and confident like some of the men she works with, but she just sees them as condescending assholes, so it's hard

---

[5] Don't even get me started on "my other half." As if any of us are half humans!

[6] Just ask work-in-the-home parents . . . I refuse to call them stay-at-home moms because it implies they're hanging out around the house. Which is utter crap. That job would be harder for me than growing a business, speaking around the world, writing a book, and coaching hundreds of other people. I know from experience.

to want to be like them. Her male counterparts speak up without hesitation more often, even when they're less qualified, interrupting her when she does gather the courage to speak. She's interested in leadership positions, but she's apprehensive about whether she'd be able to pull it off. She doesn't feel confident in her abilities, despite the fact that she's well educated and experienced.

On top of all this, she's still single and childless, and people wonder why. Is she dating anyone? When is she going to get married and have kids? Where are those grandchildren she's supposed to have in order to please her parents? But she hasn't found the right person for her yet. She doesn't know if she wants marriage or kids. Doesn't know whether she'd even be able to juggle it all at once without failing spectacularly or having to give up the career she worked so hard for. While observing her male peers, she recognizes she contributes at least as much, but she's getting paid less and knows it. And if she, at some point, decides to create human life, she vomits between meetings and falls into bed at 6:30 p.m. more exhausted than she has ever been, only to be woken up by sore hips, heartburn, and an alien in her stomach who's convinced 3:00 a.m. is an ideal time to throw a dance party. When said alien makes its debut, it comes with stitches, hemorrhoids, rock-hard breasts, and sleep deprivation that makes her feel constantly drunk, minus the fun parts. If her child refuses to latch, loses weight, or if her breasts under- or over-produce milk, the "most natural thing in the world" may create tears of utter despair as she questions whether she was even meant to be a mother in the first place. She feels judgment from all directions, and that doesn't even remotely compare to the internal guilt she places on herself should she even consider keeping her tiny human alive in any way that's "not natural." God forbid using a bottle. And, of course, she needs more than three months of maternity leave to feel like she has any idea what she's doing, but she worries she'll be judged no matter what she chooses. Going back to work too early means she must not be maternal, but going back too late means she's not committed to her career. If she goes back and doesn't sob when she leaves her child, she's heartless. If she goes back and sobs her eyes out, she's emotional. "Seriously, get your shit together, lady. It's not like you performed a goddamn miracle or anything!" Except she did. And when she does go back to work, Dick (short for Richard) asks if she enjoyed her time off. *No, Dick. I wasn't on a fucking vacation. I just got back from the hardest and most important time of my life—and trust me, there was no pool service. Don't think it's a big deal?!? You fucking do it, Dick.*[7] *Because I seem to remember you being out of the office for three days for a tummy ache. I'd love to see you push a bowling ball out of your vagina or have major surgery and then "recover" by keeping a tiny human alive.*

And then, maybe, she decides to create life again—one, two, three more times...maybe even more if she's ridiculously brave. She may decide to work inside the home; she may have that choice.

---

[7] Moral of the story: #DontBeARichard.

She might feel forced into it because the cost of daycare is about the same as what her or her partner makes, but everyone assumes she'd be the one to stay home regardless. She may instead go back to work because she feels like it's part of her purpose. Either way, she'll start saying things like, "I couldn't imagine being away from my kids all day," or "Working makes me a better mom," because she feels compelled to explain her choice, as if it's anyone else's business.

Mind you, the pressure to be pretty and sexy hasn't gone anywhere. Only a few short weeks after pushing out something that took nine months to grow, she's trying to get her body to "bounce back" to its former glory.[8] She can't let herself go, lest her husband's eyes start to wander. Should he cheat or leave her, she'll question if it's because she wasn't sexy enough, or was too tired to meet his needs, or failed in some other way like not being able to do it all. Nobody would say anything to her face, but behind closed doors there would be whispers of her failings, and she knows it. She'd be judged regardless of what she chose among the multitude of other available options like communication, therapy, or even divorce. Divorce would inspire all the same judgment and whispers anyway, so it's not like she can really win here.

Ask me again why women lack confidence. Maybe my rant wasn't enough for you? I repeat: How the fuck could we not?!

---

[8] Which is just ridiculous because it's the only instance I've ever heard where someone tries to go back to pre-miracle status after performing one. I never read anything about Mary wanting to get her pre-virgin-birth body back.

You might be reading through this and thinking, "That story isn't true for everyone," or "It's not like that anymore," or "That wasn't my experience growing up." If *none* of this speaks to your experience, that's amazing and I want to bestow a medal of honor onto your parents, family, community, bosses, and spouse (if you have one). Medals all around! Can they teach courses?! Unfortunately, you would be the exception, not the norm. I promise you there are women who are experiencing some or all of this. I talk to them. I hear their stories. I am them.

On the other hand, you might be reading this and thinking I only scratched the surface of many women's experiences, and you'd be right. I didn't mention anything about race, culture, religion, sexual orientation, gender identity, poverty, access to healthcare, overcoming sexual assault, domestic violence, or the many other contributors that can factor into the experience of being a woman. I'd argue that my rant only touched on a few challenges because addressing all of them would fill multiple books. There are women who haven't experienced any of what I've talked about, but not many. For most of us, mixed messages are everywhere. Misogyny is everywhere.

The reality is that while we've made great progress, we still have a long way to go. Women face particular challenges in relation to confidence due to the influence of patriarchy, socialization, gender-based expectations, and many other factors. We've been taught a number of self-limiting lies about ourselves, our value, and our abilities, and those lies frequently hold us back from becoming the people we truly want to be. The system is working against us. It negatively impacts men as well—but what we're working against was not created by or for us in the first place, even if many of us collectively bought into it and continue to reinforce it. In this chapter, I'm going to focus on evidence of how the confidence con plays out in our everyday lives and how we can approach the knowledge we have about it with fresh insight.

THE CONFIDENCE GAP BETWEEN THE SEXES

The example given in my rant is pseudo-fictional but echoes an all-too-common experience backed up by countless real-world statistics. A 2003 Cornell University study, which founded the renowned Dunning-Kruger effect, showed men tend to substantially overestimate their abilities and performance while women underestimate both, even when their actual performance at work doesn't differ in quality or quantity. In another well-known study, Hewlett Packard found that male employees were likely to apply for promotions when they felt they met 60 percent of the qualifications listed, while its female employees were likely to apply only when they believed they met 100 percent of the job qualifications. While women's confidence increases with age, as I mentioned at the beginning of this chapter, the data begs the question: How many opportunities are women missing out on due to a lack of confidence during the first three to four decades of their careers?

There are people who might posit that the confidence gap is a result of women being less educated or qualified for their careers as a whole, but further stats prove otherwise. The National Center for Education Statistics reports that women have outnumbered men on college campuses since 1988. They've earned more bachelor's, master's, and doctoral degrees than men since then. Women also have an immense influence on the economy, as they direct 83 percent of all consumption in the U.S. through both buying power and influence and are the principal shoppers in 72 percent of households, according to a 2019 report by Morgan Stanley. You would think women would recognize our personal and professional power, yet we still show up as less confident than men in the professional world.

I have no beef with masculinity. Frankly, I have a lot of masculine qualities, and because of that, I've found it a little easier than most to navigate many professional environments. I recognize, from personal experience, the privilege my traditionally masculine qualities afford. My beef is that most work environments have over-rotated toward valuing the masculine so much that feminine qualities like empathy, listening, and collaboration are often missing from company cultures. This imbalance leads to retention, development, and leadership issues, among others. Do I believe in hard work, being decisive and ambitious, taking risks, and being independent? You bet your ass I do. But I don't believe *only* in those things. Our obsession with grit, grind, success at all costs, the lone-wolf mentality, and demonstrating power over others has a cost. That cost is that we undervalue and underutilize traditionally feminine skills in everyone. I advocate for authenticity, acceptance, and celebration of people's strengths.

It's not just women who are feeling the pressure to perform, emphasize their masculine traits, and downplay their feminine ones. Men feel this pressure, too. They limit "soft" emotions, lean hard into the qualities that will help them be accepted within company cultures, and feel pressure to prioritize professional success over everything else. They disconnect with many of the amazing feminine qualities in others, but also within themselves. The takeaway here is that any time you become separated from any part of your authentic self, you lose trust.

WOMEN AND IMPOSTER SYNDROME

While I don't consider myself an expert on imposter syndrome, it's a subject I've been asked to cover at oh-so-many speaking engagements. It's a real problem for a significant number of people; and chances are, you've felt it at some point, too. In 2011, *The Journal of Behavioral Science* published a study that estimated 70 percent of the population, male and female, had wrestled with this problem before, but that it impacted women and people of color at a higher rate. Because we're underrepresented in leadership positions, we're short on mentors, role models, and bosses we'll be able to closely relate to. This shortage creates isolation and the feeling we don't belong, which acts as a barrier that has us questioning whether we can trust ourselves.

Throughout my coaching work, I've noticed that, as is the case with the word "confidence," people have a tendency to both over-use and misuse "imposter syndrome." We throw it out there anytime we're feeling anxious or nervous, having doubts, or are feeling bad at work. The reality is that those feelings are *normal* to experience in some contexts, especially when we're trying something for the first time. We should expect to feel butterflies and have questions and doubts while learning new things. This doesn't signify imposter syndrome.

Imposter syndrome, according to experts I've spoken with on the subject, is when we regularly internalize our mistakes and exter-nalize our successes. If something goes wrong, we say things like, "I messed up. I'm a bad communicator. I suck. I'm a horrible leader. I dropped the ball." We think *we* are the problem. If something goes right, however, we say things like, "I got lucky. It was good timing. My team are the real heroes. I just know the right people," or even, "I was blessed." In these cases, we credit outside forces for our successes and never acknowledge our achievements as our own. If this sounds like your M.O., and if you consistently doubt your abilities despite all the evidence to the contrary, imposter syndrome may be at play.

When it comes to defining imposter syndrome, the fear of being "found out" is also in the mix. We worry we'll be discovered and exposed as a fraud, like I used to do before I discovered the real meaning of confidence. "I can't do this. I'm in over my head and someone's going to notice." This worry usually relates to our job or a role we're working to fulfill, but it can play out at home as well. Women striving to be the perfect mother or spouse can suffer equally from worries that they don't know what they're doing and will be called out for it someday. Make a mistake? "I'm a horrible mom!" Do something well? "Oh, well, they got that from their dad."

Our culture often puts the onus of imposter syndrome on the person suffering from the condition. While I believe we're all responsible for our own thoughts and feelings, I also know that our environment does contribute to this issue. A sense of belonging fosters confidence, while feeling that we don't belong can harm it. When we're stuck in a toxic situation—like a boys' club environment, one where new team members are shamed for their lack of experience, or one where employee sales numbers are written out for all to see— we feel additional pressure to measure up that we might not feel otherwise. And sometimes, we really are just surrounded by jerks!

Think about it like this: we can approach new endeavors with confidence in ourselves, even if we don't have confidence in our current level of ability. If I start a new job or take on a new role, *of course* I'll be nervous that I don't know everything I need to excel and don't know for sure that I'll be great at it. However, I can trust that I'll figure it out as I go, and that I'll be OK no matter what. It would help all of us to keep in mind that even the most experienced and successful people have doubts, fears, failures, and missteps.

Women across the world are experiencing imposter syndrome in their personal and professional lives, regardless of position, status, income, or success. The solution is to develop lasting confidence that comes from within, so that in all experiences, good or bad, we can acknowledge our role and trust ourselves to bring our unique strengths, abilities, and talents to the table.

COMPETENCE VS. CONFIDENCE

Nobody questions whether my husband is a good spouse or father—and he absolutely is—despite the fact that he works full-time like I do. People are frequently enamored by how engaged he is as a dad. "It's so nice he shares pick-up and drop-off at school!" No one's ever been enamored by how engaged I am as a mom. If anything, people question whether I'm doing enough and possibly forcing my husband to pick up the slack. "She's so driven! It's so sweet how much he supports her!" Because women are judged across a wider scope, we encounter more areas in life where our ability to build confidence is hindered and impeded. Plenty of stats back this up. The University of Kent published a 2019 study that showed men are judged at work by their leadership *potential* while women are judged on their past performance. We're not given the benefit of the doubt like they are and feel we have to go the extra mile to prove ourselves. We also tend to feel like our mistakes carry more weight than they do—and, unfortunately, the data shows it's true more often than not. No wonder we constantly doubt ourselves and think something is wrong with us!

As women, our solution to this problem has been to over-rotate on competence. We think we need to get all the degrees and designations, become experts in our field as quickly as possible, and have all the answers in every situation. We think if we're totally competent at what we do, then we'll finally feel confident and get the recognition, compensation, and respect we deserve. I wish that worked. Unlike the chicken and the egg, there is no question which skill comes first. Competence is built over time, meaning you can't be competent at anything when you first start. Confidence, however, you can have any time you want, so it comes first. Competence can increase our confidence and will build over time as we hone our skills and become better at whatever we're trying to do. But waiting to be confident *until* we feel competent is creating far too many barriers for women.

This over-rotation on competence is standing in our way. Of course, it's important to get educated, increase knowledge, and improve at the work we do over time, but obsessively zeroing in on it limits us from seeing the bigger picture. We need to be able to take risks, try new things, and make changes without feeling scared that we won't perform perfectly. Conversely, men tend to over-rotate on confidence, applying for jobs they're not fully qualified for and overestimating their performance and abilities at work. They lead with confidence and are therefore more willing to take leaps of faith.

Men and women have a lot to learn from each other in this area. The answer to over-rotation on either side is not to lean all the way into confidence or competence exclusively, but to begin with confidence while on the road to competence and to eventually balance both. This is crucial if women are ever going to see equal representation in leadership positions, because research shows that when given a choice, people will follow the most confident person in the room. This is true when their competence is equal to that of others present *and* when it's unequal. Said another way, if one person is more confident than another, people will follow him even if he's the less-competent one. This may seem ridiculous,[9] but if you had to follow somebody, wouldn't you trust the person who trusts themselves? If you were lost in the woods with a friend who was positive they knew the way home and a former ranger who didn't quite know which way to head, you'd follow your friend, right? Anything to make it back to civilization!

If men and women learned from each other and cut back on over-rotation surrounding the confidence-competence divide, I believe we'd all be in much better shape. We'd have more qualified leaders, better communication skills, and greater representation for women in various spheres. If you're reading this and suspect you currently lean into competence too hard, know that choosing confidence is the road to balance.

---

[9] It is ridiculous and makes me crazy, but it's also our current reality.

IT'S OKAY TO BE ANGRY . . . WE'VE EARNED IT

The reason you probably don't have the confidence you could as a woman is because you were never set up to win. The limitations we were raised with, combined with everything else discussed in this chapter, are real and often infuriating. If you have strong emotions about the oppression women experience, you're not alone. It makes perfect sense to be upset about the system we were born into. Unfortunately, women are judged more harshly than men for expressing anger and other "hard" emotions in our day-to-day lives. This harsher judgment tends to fracture our confidence even further, but it doesn't have to. In the next chapter, we're going to talk all about anger and the other tough emotions we have to navigate on a regular basis, if not daily, and how they relate to the work of building confidence.

CHAPTER 3

Reconciling Confidence with Strong Emotions

"You may encounter defeats, but you must
not be defeated. In fact, it may be necessary to encounter
the defeats, so you can know who you are, what you
can rise from, how you can still come out of it."

—MAYA ANGELOU

DO ALL THE DOUBLE STANDARDS, the need to constantly prove ourselves by doing more and performing better, and the inequities in pay make me angry? You bet they do. Maybe anger isn't the emotion you feel when you read about issues like sexism and patriarchy. Maybe it's sadness, frustration, defensiveness, disappointment, confusion, a sense of being overwhelmed, or even judgment. My point is that many of us have strong feelings about these issues, whatever they may be, and that's natural.

So what do strong, difficult feelings like these have to do with our ability to be confident? Far too much.

Anger is an emotion I tend to feel quite a lot. My father has always had a fiery personality, which I inherited. For a long time, it impacted my confidence in ways I didn't know how to navigate. I struggled to handle my anger because expressing it always seemed to result in punishment from society, colleagues, and people with power over my career path. I once applied for a high-level program at the company where I worked but was denied. I followed up by asking one of the guys in a decision-making seat what was holding me back from being granted that opportunity.

"Are you hearing anything about what's preventing me from making it into that program? I can't figure out the reason. I've hit all the necessary metrics."

His response? "You have some work to do on being so reactive. You should connect with Diana,[10] as she's made some real progress with managing her emotions."

Reactive. A kind way of implying my anger made me difficult to work with.

To be fair, he wasn't wrong. I did have some work to do in that area and was willing to accept his feedback. What pissed me off, however, was knowing at least five men who'd made it into that program had a reputation throughout the enterprise for their "reactive"

---

[10] (Not her real name.)

personalities. If showing anger was the differentiator between being offered or denied a seat at the table, none of them should've gotten in, either. I also loathed that he suggested I connect with one of the very few other women in the same position as me to work on "my emotions" versus the mass population of men who also needed to work on the same issue.

That decision-maker had ultimately conveyed a version of the message women around the world receive every day: expressing anger or any "strong emotion" was unbecoming specifically due to my sex and would prevent me from accomplishing my goals. I share this story as an example of how society uses our anger against us, but it wasn't the first time I'd dealt with this issue. As a result of being ostracized for this natural emotion I happen to have a lot of, I spent years trying to soften myself and shove my anger down. It developed into an obsession with self-control that became a full-fledged eating disorder. I did anything and everything I could to curb and purge my anger, even though I hadn't stopped feeling it.

Women have a number of things to be rightfully angry about, but are told from a young age that showing it is unacceptable. No one shrugs off our anger while saying "Girls will be girls." No one deems us strong, firm, or assertive when we let it out. Instead, our anger is perceived as a character failing and we're gaslit, ignored, belittled, questioned, and shouted down in response. I've heard from so many Black women that they can't express emotions that are even anger-adjacent, lest they get tagged with the label of "angry

Black woman." And I can't think of a community of women with a more legitimate reason to be angry. Latinas' anger gets called feisty or fiery, which effectively minimizes and brands it as "cute." These reactions can cause us to question ourselves, even in cases where our anger is justified, and elicit people-pleasing habits. This separates us from our authentic feelings and fractures our trust in ourselves, damaging our confidence if we let it—but I've learned it doesn't have to. In fact, when we approach anger from an authentic and responsible place, we can leverage it to fortify our confidence.

GENDER STEREOTYPES DENY OUR EMOTIONAL SPECTRUM

All humans experience the full spectrum of emotion, from anger to sadness to happiness to fear. The feelings that are seen as acceptable for us to express, however, were determined by gender stereotypes that existed before any of us were born. Men are allowed hard emotions like anger, but not softer, vulnerability-laden ones like sadness. They're berated and told to "man up" if they cry. Women, on the other hand, get called "difficult" if we dare let our anger be known. None of us are freely allowed to feel or demonstrate *all* the different parts of who we are. We're told to either follow the script or suffer the consequences.

There's nothing wrong with soft emotions like sadness. The problem is that when something hard happens in our lives, soft emotions are incongruent to the situation. Hard happens, frequently, and it's natural that hard emotions come with it. If someone punched me in the face while walking down the street, I might feel a variety of emotions—but being pissed off would definitely be high up in the mix. It'd be a bit strange if it wasn't, no? When we're not allowed the specific emotions that match specific experiences, our ability to process and get through them is limited. We think there's something wrong with us and beat ourselves up for feeling those forbidden emotions in the first place. We try to ignore that internal voice telling us we feel something, and our confidence suffers as a result. We lose trust.

Through therapy and the confidence-building work I've done, I've come to believe my anger is valid simply *because it's there*. It's OK to own all my feelings as long as they aren't owning *me*.

I've learned that denying ourselves a difficult emotion only ends up creating more problems, which is the opposite of what we want. What you resist persists. My coach, Lisa Kalmin, taught me this and so much more. In fact, anyone who's health-oriented will tell you that holding in feelings like sadness or anger rather than processing and releasing them creates stress. The hormones generated by this stress, in turn, can manifest in the form of depression, anxiety, panic attacks, colds and viruses, circulatory problems, and more. It creates a vicious cycle leading to more stress. More anger. More depression. This cycle isn't just harmful to us as individuals, but also to our interpersonal relationships and society as a whole. It benefits no one to have large numbers of people trying to make their way through life on the edge of exploding or having a breakdown. Pushing away the feelings we don't like does nothing to solve the problems causing them. Our emotions have to go somewhere, and if we're not mindful about dealing with them, they remain trapped, and they fester within us. And if you don't make time for your mental, emotional, and physical wellness, you'll end up needing to make time for your illness.

You'll never get to a point of only feeling emotions you like or being able to block them all out entirely. Humans don't work that way. When we don't let ourselves experience all our emotions to the fullest, however they come, we send the message to our subconscious that there are parts of ourselves we can't trust. You may as well build a brick wall between yourself and your confidence, because to be truly confident, we need to trust our entire selves. Remember, confidence is knowing who you are, owning who you're not, and choosing to embrace *all* of it.

DEALING WITH ANGER IN WAYS
THAT BUILD CONFIDENCE

You might be feeling stuck about the best way to handle your own anger or whatever tough emotions you may experience. *What if I express it and people don't like it?* I'm not a therapist, but I do know what's effective for me and the many women I work with, and it allows us to propel toward the best version of ourselves: a shift in mindset.

I now trust myself to know that I'm allowed to have any emotion that comes up and get to decide what to do with it, and that I'll be able to handle whatever consequences stem from my decision. There are always consequences for your choices. For every action, there's a reaction, whether it's good, bad, or indifferent. It's likely someone will have an opinion about my emotions. Someone else can think I'm not supposed to show up that way, but that doesn't make it true. I can't decide or choose what others think of me. At the end of the day, especially when it comes to my confidence, what matters is whether I feel proud or good about myself.

I've expressed anger in ways I'm not proud of in the past. I've gotten into arguments with friends and ex-boyfriends and said horrible, hurtful things I regretted the moment they flew out of my mouth. Reflecting on behavior we regret can feel bad, but it can also allow us to grow. Expressing anger can *build* confidence when we speak our truth responsibly and in a way that's authentic to us. If we're bothered by something that's happening and choose to stand up for ourselves, we create trust in ourselves. If someone makes a joke at our expense and then tells us they were "just kidding," we build trust in ourselves when we say there was nothing funny about it. If someone hurts us and tells us not to take it personally, it's OK to say that their actions were personal, so there's no other way to take it. When someone tells me not to be so sensitive, I can say, "That's funny. I'm not generally known for my sensitivity." Standing up for ourselves builds trust and increases confidence exponentially.

I don't know about you, but I always feel worse when I don't say what I believe or when I choose not to speak up when I feel I should. I could line up pages of examples where not speaking up chipped away at my own trust, all because I allowed myself to sit through them quietly and effectively condone someone else's bad behavior.

I shouldn't have laughed at that joke. That was hurtful.

He shouldn't have talked to her like that. Why didn't I tell him how inappropriate he was being?

I had every right to express my boundaries at that moment. Why didn't I?

These were learning experiences that allowed me to get clear about the fact that my anger, discomfort, and hurt feelings were my gut telling me that something didn't feel right. When we make a habit of owning our emotions to the fullest, we get the opportunity and benefit of feeling proud of how we choose to handle them. We get to decide when and how we want to show our anger to others; when to say something and when to walk away; when to spend that energy and when to conserve it; and when it's worth it to us and when it's not. No one else is entitled to make those calls. Trusting ourselves enough to handle those moments is all about getting in touch with our authentic selves and using that connection to foster our own integrity.

CHOOSING INTEGRITY OVER PEOPLE-PLEASING

So many of us get into the habit of working to please everyone but ourselves because we think making other people happy will feel good and benefit us. We want to be likable rather than rock the boat. We believe advantages will come to us if the recipients of our people-pleasing like us. The unfortunate reality is that it's rarely possible to prioritize living in our truth when our main focus is getting others to like us. You're going to have to choose one or the other the vast majority of the time. Every time you're people-pleasing, someone else may like you more, but you are going to end up liking and trusting yourself less. It's a lovely feeling when others recognize how awesome we are, but it only has substance when our good deeds are coming from a place of integrity. Choosing to prioritize living your truth actually has the added benefit of attracting the people who are the right fit for you, so that's something to consider. If you're not prioritizing yourself, you're probably sacrificing your own pleasure and happiness for others, and you're probably attracting people who are happy to take advantage of that.

The word "integrity," by the way, is one I avoided in my twenties. At the company where I worked, we'd get the entire organization together on a regular basis to discuss questions like, "What are our values? What do we stand for? What's our mission?" The people around me working in financial services would inevitably answer, "Integrity." But I was adamantly opposed to listing that as a core value, probably because I wasn't living it in my own life. As it turns out, however, there are two definitions attached to the word. The first is, "the quality of being honest and having strong moral principles and moral uprightness." That sounds great and all, but it didn't resonate with me because I had to question who got to decide the morals we were using as our standard in business. Are morals about being ethical and honest when dealing with clients? Obviously. Do they mean not lying, stealing, or otherwise doing harm to my company? I would think so. But does it also mean that a woman can't bring a date, unless it's her spouse, to an overnight work trip? (True story.) Does it mean that my work colleagues get to have an opinion about my personal choices? Are we talking about religious morals, and if so, which religion? Or are we referring to philosophical approaches to ethics? And whose ethics, values, or perspectives are being used to decide? Discussions surrounding the concept all seemed too vague and loosey-goosey to me. The second definition of integrity, however, describes "the state of being whole and undivided." It's about integrating every part of ourselves—tough emotions included—into our life so we can experience wholeness. That's a far more relatable concept for me and, as counterintuitive as it may seem, does more to boost our confidence in the long run. People-pleasers run on the belief that if they get what they want from others, they'll feel good about themselves. They think that if other people trust them, they'll be able to trust themselves and their confidence will grow in the process. This is an illusion. For the most part, the opposite is true.

Trusting yourself has to come first in order for your confidence to be real and to endure. Validation from others can be taken away from you at any point, but true confidence as we've defined it in this book is always in your hands. And when you show up authentically and other people like it, that's just icing on the cake!

How many times have you heard it said that you can't please everyone? More than you can count by now, I'm sure, and that's because it's true. You'll be too much for some people, and not enough for others. Those just aren't your people. I teach a workshop on occasion called *Who Do You Serve?* It's designed to help women narrow down their target market so they can effectively serve their ideal clients. The foundation of this workshop is the fact that we do not, cannot, and will not ever be able to serve everyone. This is marketing 101. When you try to speak to everyone, you inevitably water your message down so much that success becomes an impossibility. The clearer you are on who you're speaking to, the more successful you'll be. If you only attracted 1 percent of the US population to your business, and each of that 1 percent only invested fifty dollars in your product or service one time, you'd be a multimillionaire. Said another way, 99 percent of the population could think you're a complete hack and hate everything you do, sell, or stand for and you'd still make around $165 million dollars.

In a world where someone's bound not to like you regardless of whether you're being real or faking it, you may as well choose to express yourself authentically. There are people out there who *will* like you for you. They'll respect you for speaking your truth. They'll make space for the parts of you others might find "difficult" and value them as much as the parts that are "easy." There's a whole slew of people in the world who will see and appreciate you just as you are. And it feels good to find your people, but it's important to know that while validation from others feels good, it won't bring you any closer to your confidence. What matters is whether you trust yourself.

So far in this book, we've analyzed confidence through the lens of the female experience. We've talked about what true confidence is, the confidence gap between men and women, and how we can approach the strong emotions society tells us we shouldn't feel in order to build lasting trust for ourselves. Next, we're going to move toward embodying our working definition of confidence through practices that can help us know who we are, own what we're not, and embrace all of it. To start down this path, we're going to talk about reconnecting with what many call our "inner knowing."

PART 2

REAWAKENING CONFIDENCE

CHAPTER 4

Know Who You Are

"At the center of your being you have the answer.
You know who you are and you
know what you want."

—LAO TZU

IF YOU'VE READ THIS FAR, you know that the reasons women struggle with confidence are legitimate. Women weren't born with less of it than men. Women are not "the weaker sex."[11] We aren't hindered by some universal feminine flaw. Most of us were raised to be nice, be polite, and take care of others, which in many cases separated us from our real feelings, possibly even our purpose, and probably our authenticity. How could we not arrive at adulthood and feel confused by the throngs of experts telling us confidence is

---

[11] How anyone can understand childbirth and still believe that is beyond me. And don't get me started on when men get sick… (Insert eye-roll here.)

the key to success? How are we suddenly supposed to attain that when we've been conditioned to respond and behave differently our whole lives?

When I was at my lowest points and lacking any real confidence, I felt completely disconnected from my true self. Trying to derive my confidence from external validation had me so confused about my values and who I was in my soul that even *I* didn't know anymore. I've noticed in coaching other women on confidence-building that a lot of us share in this struggle, even though most of us believe we're the only ones who feel this way.

I look back on that now, and it's clear to me how skewed my perception was and how messed up the cultures we live in are. This is especially obvious when I think about the hatred I used to have for my own body. When I close my eyes and tune into myself to ask, *What purpose does my body serve?,* the voice that answers has a completely different take than what I'd always been told. My body is my vessel, a home, a temple in this life, and the way it looks is completely separate from its purpose. My priorities for my body are health, longevity, and strength. What I should be thinking about is whether it's nourished and honored, not starved and hated.

We're exposed to so much commentary, so many opinions, and so many voices throughout the course of our lives that it becomes challenging to hear and listen to *our* internal voice above all the others. Making a habit of listening to that voice inside me, which I call my inner knowing, was one of the most important changes I made on the road to building true confidence. This is, I believe, key if we're to accomplish the first part of what it means to be confident: knowing who you are. In this chapter, we're going to talk about that inner knowing and how to hear it, and use a specific exercise I've developed that you can use to reconnect with who you truly are. In the final part of this book, we'll get into the "how" of confidence-building, but this part is more about the "where." Where does confidence come from? The answer is easy: inside of you. We've already discussed that the messages we all receive lead to false ideas and overall misconceptions about confidence. Your confidence is unique to you; it will look and feel different than my confidence or anyone else's. When you begin to listen to and connect with your*self* again, you begin the process of rebuilding trust, which leads to real, lasting confidence. Again, it all starts with—and inside of—*you*.

WHAT IS INNER KNOWING?

Your inner knowing is what you hear when you get quiet and eliminate all the noise. It's an instinct you have that you can hear and feel in your body. You notice it when something becomes clear or obvious to you. It speaks from the core of your authentic self, and it will never lie to you about who you are. Some people might call it your gut instinct, insight, or possibly even a hunch. Others refer to this internal voice as the "higher self" or the "universal conscious-ness," or interpret it as God speaking to them from within. I don't care what you call it, only that you listen to it. Have you ever just *deeply known* what's right for you?

However you want to conceptualize it, your inner knowing is the essence of your ingrained human wisdom. You'll never be able to connect to your confidence if you're constantly questioning that voice and trying to shut it down or override it. Why? Because if you don't listen to and trust your*self*, you've put your confidence in the hands of someone or something else. Reconnecting with that source of knowing, and building a relationship with it, will serve as an unshakeable guide for all you do. You'll know you're hearing it if what it says feels right and makes sense, not necessarily in a logical way, but deep in your gut.

It may have been a while since you've heard or listened to your inner knowing. You might, in fact, be filled with and surrounded by voices saying things that are diametrically opposed to it. If that's the case for you, don't panic. Your inner knowing hasn't gone anywhere, even if you feel like you can't currently hear or feel it. Whether it's buried deep inside you or simmering just below the surface, it still lives as you live, and you'll always have access to it. Sometimes it just takes a bit of focus and faith to reconnect.

It's important to note that your inner knowing isn't every voice you hear in your mind. If you're like me, most of your mind's ongoing conversation consists of either utter nonsense ("Are gorgonzola and blue cheese the same?!"), a running task list ("Gotta swing by the bank, drop off the dry cleaning, pick up dinner... Don't forget the gorgonzola!"), or limiting, self-destructive beliefs I call "head trash" ("If I keep eating so much cheese, I'll gain twenty pounds and nobody will ever love me!"), which we'll talk about in more detail in chapter seven. You've got to be able to distinguish one voice from the other if you're going to create the opportunity to hear your inner knowing clearly. Our inner knowing speaks from a quiet, calm, connected space rooted in love, compassion, and knowledge. Head trash, on the other hand, is mean and frenetic. It tells us we can't accomplish our goals and that we're not enough as we are. It tears us down with lies rather than builds us up with truths. A good test for when you're unsure of which is speaking—head trash or your inner knowing—is to ask yourself, "Would I talk this way to someone I love, like my spouse, best friend, or child?" If the answer is no, it's not your inner knowing and you should stop saying it to yourself.

RECONNECTING WITH YOUR*SELF*

In coaching, as well as in therapy, the best of the best won't tell you what to do. They ask questions to help uncover and reveal *your* answers because they operate under the assumption that what you need already exists inside you. The problem isn't that your inner knowing isn't there; it's that you—like most people—have become disconnected from it. Many of us find ourselves defining who we are based on the opinions, feedback, and beliefs of others because we've forgotten, or were never told in the first place, that we are the only deciders of who we are and the purpose we serve. You might be thinking, "Hold on. God has a plan for me, so He is the decider." If you're religious, I can see where you're coming from, but let's agree that God lives *within* you. Even if you believe it's God that's speaking and deciding, that voice would be internal. I'm not particularly religious, but I have read the Bible cover to cover, and that's my interpretation of it. But again, you're the decider for you. What I believe is that we didn't enter this world disconnected from ourselves. Babies aren't confused about their purpose. They aren't constantly second-guessing themselves. They communicate their needs and desires without hesitation. The question in my mind is, how do we find our way back to that place?

There are many ways we can reconnect with our true selves—some of which you've probably already heard of or experienced personally, like journaling, meditation, practicing gratitude, spending time in nature, creating, praying, or deep breathing. My personal favorite, however, is an activity I've developed and used in my coaching sessions called "The Things I Know to Be True About Me, at This Point in My Life." Yes, I'm aware that's an obnoxiously long title for an exercise, but each word is important here. By identifying what we know to be true about ourselves, what we believe and trust, we can create an internal framework to live authentically. If, for example, you've grown up being told good women are quiet and submissive, but you value direct communication, and contributing your input is important to you, how do you reconcile those two ways of being? Through this activity, you'll be able to hear the opinions, feedback, and external messaging of others and begin to run it through the filter of "Does that ring true for me?" For instance, if someone said some bullshit to me like, "A woman's place is in the home," I'd instantly run it through my "Things I Know To Be True About Me…" filter and think, "That doesn't resonate at all. That isn't true for me. That's not who I am." I'd let it go (after a snarky comment, perhaps) and move on with confidence—trusting in myself—rather than spending another second entertaining the nonsense. In this way, I've saved myself hours, days, and even weeks of precious time that I used to waste on overthinking and taking everything personally.

The second part of this activity's title, the "at this point in my life" portion, is equally important. We are growing, learning, constantly-evolving beings. How we see ourselves will progress in response to our experiences, successes, and failures. What you know to be true about yourself will grow and evolve right along with you, and that's as it should be. You'll learn new things about *you*. (Keeps things kinda interesting right?)

OK, so you're probably asking *how* do I do this? Here are the five steps to creating your own "Things I Know To Be True About Me, at This Point in My Life" list:[12]

---

[12] If you'd like a pretty template to write or type on, you can download one for free on my website: nicolekalil.com/things-i-know-to-be-true-about-me.

Step 1: Start by making a list of things you know to be true about you, at this point in your life.

The first step in making your list is to create some time when you can be alone, ideally with no or minimal distractions. Thirty minutes will work, but an hour is even better. You could even take a full day and make it a self-care retreat. I'll give you a standing O! Bring a notebook or some paper and a pen, open a notes app on your phone, or type your list into Word on your computer. Or download that free template from my website if that will help you. Whatever works for you. Don't overthink it.

Take five deep breaths. Do anything that grounds you. For example, you might close your eyes, plant your feet firmly on the ground, open your arms, and say a prayer or mantra. Ask yourself—out loud, if you're brave—*"What do I know about me?"* Write down anything that comes to your mind without evaluating, questioning, or judging it. Nobody needs to see this list and you'll have the opportunity to edit it later. This is not the time to reflect on your thoughts. This is just a time to be open to what you receive. Your brain might go, "Oh no, not that," or "Eh, you're only that some of the time," or "So-and-so is much more *that* than you are." That is *not* the voice you want to be listening to. If that voice shows up, calmly acknowledge it and set it aside. Maybe even say, "Hello, head trash. I know I listen to you a lot, but not today." Then take a few more deep breaths and refocus on the amazing things you know to be true about yourself.

Things that you can count on. Things you like and appreciate about yourself. Your superpowers. Write them all down.

Here are a few questions to help you get the gears turning if coming up with a good list of things you know to be true about you feels challenging:

What do I like about myself?

What can I count on about myself? What do others trust about me?

What seems to come more naturally to me than to others?

What gives me energy? What do I feel passionate about?

What do I do well or with ease?

What positive feedback am I consistently given that rings true to me?

If I had a superpower, what would it be?

What are my gifts and talents?

What makes me different?

What draws people to me?

I've done this exercise enough times, with enough women, to tell you that the average number of things people put on their list is six. Now, there's no right or wrong number. You could end up with one powerful, amazing thing that covers you completely, and that would be great. But in my experience, women don't come up with more things for their list because they literally can't think of any more great things about themselves. This is because we're completely out of practice. We don't want to come across as arrogant, even to ourselves, and we've been conditioned to focus more on others. Don't believe me? I've asked women to create a list for the people they love most in their life, like their partner, child, or parent. The average number on those lists? Thirty-two, in twenty minutes. So, indulge me here. *You* are a complex and valuable being. How do I know that? Because you're here. As the Bible says, you were fearfully and wonderfully made with great reverence, heartfelt interest, and respect. There has never been another you in history, and there will never be another you ever again. You've lived years, experienced highs and lows, victories and heartbreaks, love and pain … and you are here. So don't you dare try to tell me there isn't more to you than the small handful of things you wrote down. I'm not buying it. You shouldn't, either. I'm going to challenge you to keep asking yourself the questions and trying to get to somewhere between thirty and fifty items on your list. This is much easier to do when you don't judge, overthink, or question everything that pops into your mind.

Of course, there are a ton of other questions you can ask yourself, but what I listed above is hopefully a good starting point. If you're anything like me, examples help. I'm not good with "blank slate" creation; I'm much more a color-by-numbers artist. So, to give you a sense of what a "Things I Know To Be True About Me …" list might look like, here's a handful of statements from my own list:

I love my people. Full stop. No negotiations.
I'm loyal.
I say what I mean and mean what I say.
I'm honest.
I'm a logical thinker and can use that to recover quickly during tough times.
I'm a good decision maker.
I impact others positively and am willing to get
uncomfortable for their benefit.
I trust my gut.
My instincts are worth listening to.
I see things, problem-solve, and find solutions quickly.
I live, love, and speak authentically.

Those are some examples from a much bigger list. You may have some or none in common with mine, but whatever you write down, make sure they all ring true for you. This is an opportunity to practice listening to that inner knowing instead of all the voices of everyone else.

One other point to make here: if you believe something about your physical appearance is a strength of yours, feel free to add it to your list. However, I'd encourage you to consider if this is something *you* know to be true about yourself versus something based on other people's opinions. "I'm pretty" or "I'm sexy" can go on your list if *you* feel pretty or sexy, and if those things are important to you, regardless of what anyone else thinks. I'd also invite you to dig a little deeper. *I have powerful thighs, I take great care of my body, I'm strong, I'm healthy, I feel pride or pleasure when I look at myself...* These may be more powerful ways to say what you know to be true about you. Clearly, I have a bias here, but if you include physical traits, I'd ask you to consider what you value about them.

Once you've got your own list to work with, I want you to go back through it and be on the lookout for any disclaimers, justifications, or wording you may be using to soften or discount any of the things you know to be true about you. I've learned in my work that we have a hard time writing, saying, or believing exclusively good things about ourselves. Most of us have been taught it's unattractive or unladylike to boast or brag, as if we're in danger of our egos taking over; we have a tendency to minimize our awesomeness, even when no one's asking us to. For example, I told you I'm a good decision maker. When this idea popped into my head, my brain said, "I'm a good decision maker most of the time," but I went back and crossed that "most of the time" out afterward. None of us are anything 100 percent of the time. This is not about perfectionism. You might write down something like, "I love to read but don't do it enough." Chuck that last part in the trash. You might write, "I'm pretty smart." Cross out the "pretty." You're just smart, and it's OK to own it. Your brain might think, "Yeah, I'm smart, but I'm not as smart as so-and-so." This isn't about comparing yourself to others. You can still be smart without being the smartest person in the world. If you find yourself including qualifiers as you make your list, set them aside and let your statements stand on their own. Make sure it reads from a confident place. Hint: qualifiers can often be hard to see on our own list. If you do this activity with a trusted friend or loved one, they'll probably be better able to see when you're doing this!

Step 2: Grow your list.

As a next step in this exercise, you're going to grow your list. One way to do so is to ask for feedback from people who both know you *and* love you (or, at the very least, respect or appreciate you). What do they know to be true about you? Asking them is a great way to add things to your list that you might not be able or willing to see about yourself. On top of that, the people who know and love you are unlikely to saddle you with the disclaimers we put on ourselves. Here are some great questions to ask, but feel free to do this in whatever way works for you:

If you had to choose my best three or four qualities, what would they be?

What do you feel like you can always count on me for?

What are my strengths or superpowers?

If you could learn anything from me, what would it be?

If I were interviewing for a job, what are the things that would make me the most hirable?

Why do you trust me?

What are your favorite things about me?

What makes me different?

Pro tip on this: consider emailing or texting these questions so people have some time to think and respond. That way, neither they nor you will have to feel awkward or put on the spot. Or, send the questions in advance and then find a time to discuss. Also, the only things you should say in response are questions like "Can you give me an example of that?" or statements like "Thank you." Do *not* try to argue with others about your badassery. It may feel uncomfortable. There may be tears. Embrace it and let it all in. If you want to give back to your loved ones, answer some of these questions for them, too, so they can also feel like a rockstar.

Once you have their answers, you can go through and decide whether you want to add each one to your list. If, for example, you don't consider yourself a funny person, but all of your friends are telling you you're funny, it probably belongs there with your own answers. You get to acknowledge that about yourself for the first time. On the other hand, if you get an answer that doesn't resonate with you, you can take interest in the fact that someone thinks that about you, but you don't have to internalize it. Other people's opinions are not the point. This is about your understanding of what you know about yourself. You're the decider, no one else.

Step 3: Review previous versions. (Skip this step if this is your first time doing anything like this.)

After you've built a list you feel good about, pull out any previous versions you've written in the past and compare them to what you have now. Is there anything you missed? Anything you wrote in the past and forgot about that should be on the current version? Also notice, has anything evolved? Are there any new things you know to be true about you now that you've experienced and learned more? This is a great time to acknowledge how you're growing.

Step 4: Read and reflect on the awesomeness that is you.

Now it's time to reread your list all the way through and reflect. How do you feel about this person you're reading about? Does your brain start listing all the things that you're *not*? Does it start to cycle through the "Yeah, but"s? Do you automatically start thinking of all your faults? If so, know that none of the things you *are* can be changed by the things that you're *not*. None of your faults change anything on your list. It is who you are. What would happen if you showed up in your life as this person consistently? What would be possible in your life if you operated fully as this person? What would be different? What would be *better*? As you reflect, you'll be able to identify areas in your life where you may not be showing up as this person. You can ask yourself *why*, in that relationship or that specific situation, you're not showing up as your true, confident self. Is it time to make some changes? Beyond all of that, this list becomes something you can read every morning before you start your day so you're walking out the door (or into your home office) filled up with the things you know to be true about you. Read and reflect as needed!

Step 5: Apply, use, practice . . . and update!

Finally, Step 5 is to apply, use, and practice the things on your list in your daily life. You might tape it to your mirror and read it every morning. Maybe you bring it out and read it before a big meeting or an important conversation. It can be a great resource when you have big, important decisions to make or during a life transition. For example, if you're thinking about applying for a promotion or leaving your job, read your list. Getting married or divorced? Read your list. Having or adopting a child, or having your youngest leave for college? Read your list. Trying to determine whether someone or something is healthy for you? Read your list. Get the idea? Your list won't do you much good if it gets lost in a file somewhere. How can you leverage it and make the most of the information you've gathered? You might even give your list to a friend or family member. When you're having a tough day or feeling disconnected from yourself, they can pull it out and read it to you. This activity is simply a tool, so use it when and how you feel it will benefit you.

Like you, your list is a living and growing thing, so make sure it evolves as you do. I typically recreate my list once a year on my birthday. I also set aside time to do this to build my confidence at major milestones, or during periods of transition when I need clarity to make a decision or courage to take a bold risk. You might recreate your list when you've landed a new job, entered into a new relationship, moved to another city, or any time you feel you're on shakier ground than usual. It's a concrete way to see your qualities listed on a page and think, "Yep, that's who I am," so you know what you can count on and who you can trust. (You. The answer is you.) There are so many ways you might incorporate it into your life, so how are you going to use all the things you know to be true about yourself?

Bonus Step: Allow me to re-introduce myself!

Put your big girl pants on and tell someone *who you are!* Not what you do for a living (boring!) or the many roles you play (exhausting!), but your superpowers, your gifts, and your talents. In short, what makes you, *you* (wildly interesting and compelling…and if someone doesn't like it? Not. Your. People).

We don't know what challenges we'll encounter in the future, but our trust for ourselves and the things we can count on are within our control and can get us through the tough times with a healthy mindset. We all have doubts and fears. That's inevitable. Having something uplifting to fall back on in those moments allows us to be resilient and rise to the next challenges that come our way. This, in turn, reinforces our confidence with the knowledge that we've conquered seemingly impossible obstacles in the past, and we can do it again.

EVOLVING TOWARD AN EVER-MORE CONFIDENT SELF

Your trust—your inner knowing—is there inside you, I promise. Regardless of where you are, you always have the opportunity to listen and choose. You can separate the two tracks playing inside you: your authentic self versus everything else. This is your greatest ally and most important lifelong relationship. Although confidence is my personal obsession, I still have work to do to stay in touch with my inner knowing. I still doubt myself and have conflicting ideas about what it means to be a successful woman in this world, but I can also look back and see how far I've come. The version of me in my twenties didn't have any kind of relationship with her authentic self. I don't know what my inner knowing was saying at that point, because I wasn't listening. The ironic thing is that the period when I may have looked the best in the eyes of others, I felt the worst. Today, I'm the most confident I've ever been and couldn't give a shit about fitting into size-four pants.

Start listening for your inner knowing as you work your way through the chapters that follow. As we go through them, pay attention to the words that resonate with you most, and allow them to be your guiding star throughout your confidence-building journey. Keep and use what feels right for you, and feel free to set the rest aside.

ACTIVITY RECAP

- -

Things I Know To Be True About Me,
at This Point in My Life

STEP 1: Make a list of things you know to be true about you, at this point in your life.

STEP 2: Grow your list.

STEP 3: Review previous versions. (Skip this step if this is your first list.)

STEP 4: Read and reflect.

STEP 5: Apply, use, practice, and update.

BONUS STEP: Re-introduce yourself!

Give these steps a try!

CHAPTER 5

Own Who You're Not and Embrace Yourself Anyway

"When you know yourself, you are empowered.
When you accept yourself, you are invincible."

—TINA LIFFORD

NOW THAT YOU'VE LEARNED about reconnecting with your inner knowing, you can work on the first step of the definition of confidence we're using in this book: knowing who you are. In my experience in working with women, that step can be challenging, but it isn't the step that tends to trip us up most. The greatest challenges we face have more to do with steps two and three: owning what you're not and choosing to embrace all of it. Freeing ourselves from perfectionism and the lies we've been told about confidence requires that we get a clear sense not only of who we are, but also of who and what we are not, who we don't want to spend our time and energy on becoming, and the things in life that simply aren't meant for us. In this chapter, we'll talk about how to do that and still make the choice to embrace it. To embrace *all* of you.

I find that when I'm coaching women, they tend to turn this part of the confidence-building process into a beat-up session. When I ask them, "What's on your 'that's-not-me' list?" they take it as an opportunity to name all their flaws, shortcomings, and weaknesses. Oddly, I get the sense this is even easier for them than identifying what their strengths are. They say things like, "I'm not smart enough. I'm not talented enough. I'm not a good enough mother. I'm not engaged enough with my family. I'm not where I wanted to be in terms of my career. I'm too *this*, and not enough *that*." By the time they're done, they're feeling less-than and wondering what's wrong with them, and any momentum we'd built from the "Things I Know to Be True About Me..." exercise has come to a screeching halt.

I want to say right now, that's not what we're going for here. This isn't meant to be an opportunity to beat yourself up. The goal is empowerment, self-awareness, and acceptance. It's also about being lovingly real and honest with yourself, which is always a trust builder. It's about sussing out the things you're not here on this planet to do or be so you can have a healthy sense of your own desires, obstacles, and boundaries. I think of this process in the same way I think of friendships. As is true for most adult women,

I've had many friendships throughout my life, but only a handful of them are lifelong. In some cases, those friendships ended with hurt feelings and disappointment. In most cases, I can appreciate who those people were in my life during a time when I needed them. I'm grateful for them, and based on evidence, we were only meant to be in each other's lives for a season. From those friendships and experiences I subconsciously began to create a list of what I *didn't* need or want in a lifelong friend, like someone who needs to talk every day, or who isn't excited for me when I have something to celebrate; or someone who gossips about me or shares personal information with others, or who doesn't have the courage to have difficult conversations when one of us has messed up. By figuring out what I definitely wasn't looking for, I was able to narrow down and refine my vision of what I did want in a friend. Doing this helped me recognize which friends I wanted to invest love and energy in and ultimately create healthy relationships with that work for both of us. So, think of this next part as an exercise in forming a healthy relationship with yourself. In this chapter, you'll be setting yourself up to build that trust.

HONORING YOUR PURPOSE

You might be thinking, "Why should I focus on what I'm not rather than telling myself I can do and be it all?" That's a good question. There is, of course, a ton of value in believing in ourselves and our potential. However, pushing ourselves to do and be everything ends up hurting us because it's unrealistic and unachievable. We only have so much time, talent, and energy to work with. When we're focused on trying to be something we're not, we rob ourselves of the ability to focus on what really matters. We've got to figure out and prioritize what we *really* want so we can give those pursuits, desires, and passions proper time and attention. If Frida Kahlo, for example, had spent her life trying to be everything, she would never have developed expert skills as an artist or become a prolific painter. If perfectionism was her goal, she never would've painted her trademark unibrow! She accepted and painted what was, as she saw it. Anyone who's ever achieved their desired level of success has had to make decisions about which pursuits will serve their purpose and which ones will end up being a distraction.

How boring and inefficient would the world be if we were all the same? In my mind, very! I didn't come here to be anyone else; I came here to be me...the best damn me I can be. And guess what? I'm the only person who can do it. (You, too, by the way.) When it comes to owning what I'm not, there's plenty I could mention. I know, for example, that I'm not a patient person. "Patience is a virtue," they say, and that's certainly true. It's just not one of mine. I'm also not tall or a star athlete. I'll never be in the WNBA, and that's something I've accepted—easily—because it was never one of my passions, and I can see it's not part of my purpose. We all have things we know we're not, as well as things that are easy for us to accept. Where it gets tricky is when we don't know what we're not, or even more likely, when those things are not easy for us to accept. As an example, accepting that intelligence may not be your gift is not easy. I know an abundant number of parents that do just about everything they can to ensure their kids are smart. Why? Because our culture puts a premium on it, and probably because they themselves experienced feeling unintelligent at some point, or at many points, during their own educational experiences. I'm sure our school system has failed many people, but I'm also sure we're surrounded every day by people who aren't smart in the traditional academic sense. It's painful to consider, but intelligence may not be your or your child's gift. Because of this, *so* many people over-rotate, overcompensate, and turn themselves inside out to prove they're smart. And in the process, they may miss out on developing their unique gifts! For the record, I own that I'm never going to be the smartest. I'm a decent test taker and figured out how to get by in school with good grades on minimal effort, but my IQ and SATs have never had anyone banging down my door.

Here's a more personal example: I can be polarizing. People either like me or they don't, but likeability and charisma have not ever, and will never be, my superpowers. I spent years fighting this, thinking it was a major design flaw, and trying so hard to be likable. I did my best to be nice, sweet, and bubbly. I attempted to create instant rapport, be endearing, and display oh so much energy!!!! (Multiple exclamation marks on everything!!!!) But it was exhausting and I was painfully bad at it. I had fears that I'd never be successful if everyone didn't like me, and I detest networking because I don't have that initial attraction power that draws people in. I have a friend who has this gift in spades. She's a master at her craft. I'm in awe, but being around her has also made it obvious that I don't share the same strengths. Jay likes to joke around that when he meets people who say, "Oh, I've met your wife! She's so sweet," he'll automatically know they've never actually met me or that they're confusing me with someone else. I'm just not that uber likable, sociable gal who makes an amazing first impression.

If you're reading this and feeling tempted to say, "Oh, no, I'm sure that's not true," or "You're really nice!" or "Don't buy into that; everyone loves you," *stop*. I can't tell you how often I own something I'm not and a woman will swoop in to try to make me feel better. The truth is, I'm totally good with this. I've embraced it. I actually like this about myself now, because in accepting it, it's allowed me to focus on what I can be really good at and what really matters to me. No, I'm not someone anyone would ever describe as sweet, but I am kind, and I take good care of the people I love. I'm never going to show up at my best in a large room of people with a desire to network, but I can build the shit out of one relationship at a time. I'm not bubbly, but I'm focused and a great listener. I can be polarizing, which means I get to find out quickly who my people are and who I shouldn't waste any more time on. Letting go of trying to be an extrovert helped me to find out how to best manage my energy as an introvert. Knowing, accepting, and embracing what I'm not, even though it was painful for many years, created the freedom I needed to double down and fully trust who I am.

I'll offer one more example that's bound to get a reaction: I'm not a "great mom." I won't be winning any Mother of the Year awards, I've never done anything Pinterest-worthy, and my lack of patience is a less-than-desirable trait in this context. Here's the real kicker, though: being the best mom isn't even a goal of mine. I don't aspire to it, don't lie awake at night thinking about it, and don't waste a lot of energy trying to win mom points with other moms. Yikes! Before someone develops a hernia, let me say that I love my daughter every second of every minute of every day. I always think about what's best for her. I provide for her, I'm there for her, and I'll protect her with my dying breath from the worst life has to offer if I can. I am an engaged mom, and I think I'm doing a pretty good job. I also wasn't sure I wanted to have a child until I did. I'm not the most maternal person you're ever going to meet, and I have never once considered leaving my career to work inside the home. I'm not your "baking sugar-free cookies with carob instead of chocolate, creating crafts and playdates, label-reading, research-gathering mom who reads parenting books and thinks her child can do no wrong or that she's my whole world." Yikes, again![13]

---

[13] Why didn't my editor talk me out of writing this?!

Now, if any of those things describe you as a mom, good for you! I'm not saying that any of this is wrong or bad. I'm just saying it's not me. Early on, I panicked when I realized that none of those things came naturally to me and that I didn't enjoy any of them. I tried for a bit to play the part, but as you now know, playing the part has never really worked out all that well for me. I can vividly remember JJ being six days old, which for me meant six days of being tormented by breastfeeding. I've literally never experienced anything that hard. She wouldn't latch, but when she did, she'd get accosted by breast milk. (I was an overproducer and didn't know it yet.) She was losing weight, I was in pain, and I dreaded the next time I'd have to attempt to feed her and then pump. I was told that it should just come naturally if you're relaxed. I was told that breastfeeding was the only way to go if I cared about my kid. (That last part was never said, but always implied.) And on the sixth day, I sobbed in my mom's arms from a place so deep I hadn't known it existed and said from a place of absolute fear, "I don't think I was meant to do this." I genuinely thought it was a sign that I wasn't supposed to be a mom, which I could just add to all the other ways I was bound to fail her because I wasn't going to do "maternal" in the way I felt and had been told I was supposed to. It took a long time, but around ten months in (coincidentally when I also stopped breastfeeding), I decided that my child had come through me, and that could not possibly have been an accident. So somehow, some way, what she needed from me was *me*. I began to think, as I often do, "What would I want for her if she was in this situation?" And what I would want for JJ, should she choose to have children, would be for her to be her best, and be herself. I'd want her to ignore all the unsolicited advice, trust that she's enough, and give the finger to anyone who had the nerve to judge her parenting or what she should do with her own breasts. So I began to model that. I'm a mom who's long on love and commitment, but short on patience. I demonstrate my love and commitment not just with her and with Jay, but in my career and with my family and friends. She didn't get the best mom; she got me.

If you don't like or agree with my approach to parenting, that's all good. I'm not here to impress anyone with my mad parenting skills. If your goal is to be a great mom, then pour yourself into it like anyone does when they want to be great at anything.[14] Great moms make the world and our future better. I'm owning that I'm not one of those moms, and embracing that my way is good enough. This makes life less stressful for me, which ironically makes me a better mom. Owning what you're not can be hard, especially if feelings of fear, shame, and guilt come along with it. But it can also be incredibly freeing and rewarding. Women haven't been taught this skill, as we're expected to just stack role upon role and skill upon skill and somehow be great at all of it. It's not healthy and it's not achievable. We need to learn the skill of acknowledging what's

---

[14] But please know that Perfect Mom is not an available option to anyone.

not for us, accepting it without judgment, and embracing it as part of what makes us great (or, at the very least, creates the space we need to focus on what makes us great).

If you have a daughter, niece, or young woman you care about, I'd ask you to consider this: we don't tell JJ she can be anything she wants. She can't. And I don't want to be there for the heartbreak and disappointment when she figures out that she's been lied to about something so important. (She'll get over Santa Claus, but this is way bigger.) I will encourage her with every fiber of my being to try new things, chase her dreams, and put effort, energy, and passion into whatever matters to her. But telling young girls that they can be whatever they want is both bullshit and problematic. What they're actually hearing when we say it is that they're supposed to do it all. They're hearing "be amazing at everything you do" and we're setting them up to fall short. We're setting them up to think there's something wrong with them, and there isn't. It's not a *them* problem; it's a society problem. And the fascinating part? JJ seems totally good with finding out she's not great at something. Her class gives out an award each week, like the "persistent award," "courageous award," or "confident award." I've asked her a few times if she thought a certain word described her and she has told me, "No, I don't think that's a good word for me," or "Yes, I am that, but I think so-and-so in my class should get that one." The week they gave out the "confident award" I secretly felt a little disappointed when she didn't get it, but that was totally a mom-projecting-onto-their-kid thing. When she won the "reliable award," she was so proud she called literally everyone in our family to tell them. She was proud of *herself*, and she told me, "I like this one. It fits me."[15]

At the end of the day, I'm never going to be the charismatic person in the room that everyone loves, and I'm never going to write a book on motherhood. I could feel bad about that, but it would hold me back from all the work I'm doing to connect women to their confidence. I could want everyone to like me, but that would make chasing my passion of eliminating gender expectations impossible. The God I believe in didn't give me the attributes and talents she did if I wasn't meant to embrace and do something with them, so I'm here to make the most of them. Whenever this life is over, I want to stand before God and say that I used every bit of the gifts I was given. I didn't waste any of it.

Before we move forward, I want to address something I briefly mentioned earlier, and that's women trying to "save" other women from owning what they're not. I see this *all the time*. If I mention a mom-fail, it's only a matter of time before someone tells me I'm a great mom or that they do worse. If a woman even hints at being bad at something, there will be a string of comments saying they're awesome at it. And a go-to response seems to be to tell women they're beautiful no matter what's going on. I know we think we're being encouraging when we do this, but what we're really doing is

---

[15] Yes, I cried. How could I not?

reinforcing the idea that confidence is given through external validation, and that women should feel good, perfect, beautiful, and awesome all the time. Please think about that the next time you feel tempted to make someone feel better by giving a generic response. And for the love of God, stop fishing for compliments by publicly bashing yourself. It may feel good temporarily, but it will do major damage to your confidence. By identifying situations in your life where you can look and say, "That's not me," you'll build confidence that will help you make the most of what you have been given, too.

OWNING WHAT WE'RE NOT BUILDS TRUST

People who struggle to own what they're not often run into difficulty when they're out of their depth, both at work and in their personal lives. We've all dealt with situations where we asked someone a question they weren't qualified or prepared to answer, like a speaker or sales rep. When they fudge their way through it and give us inaccurate or incomplete information, we end up disappointed and lose trust, right? It's way more desirable to be told, "That's not my area of expertise, so let me connect you with someone who can get you that answer." Or, "Great question! I'm not sure, so let me look into this and get back to you." Confident people don't fudge. When they don't know, they say so.

Not being able to acknowledge our limitations when we're out of our depth can have incredibly harmful consequences. Imagine being president of a country and having very little knowledge of foreign policy. Acting like you know it all could result in a war! You'd want to consult the people in your cabinet with experience in that area before making big decisions, right? Or, imagine being a doctor and treating a patient with symptoms you've never seen before. Thinking "I've got this; I can do it all myself" could end up killing them. When we trust ourselves enough to say, "I can't or shouldn't do this, at least not without support," or "I don't know the answer here, but that's OK; I'll look into it and figure it out," we give ourselves the opportunity to learn and improve. When we trust ourselves enough to say "I don't believe my product or service would be the best fit for you, but let me recommend you to someone who I think could be," we get to make space for people who are the right fit and will become raving fans, as well as the added benefit of gaining trust with the person we were honest with. We continually get better when we make owning who and what we're not into a habit. This, in turn, boosts our trust in ourselves and allows us to be more confident moving forward. The benefits of owning what we're not build on themselves over time.

Owning what we're not can also help us stay on solid ground in times of uncertainty. Take the COVID-19 pandemic, for instance. One thing I'm completely certain I'm not is an expert on the virus or how it works. When it first appeared, no one was. Frankly, as I'm writing this book, I'm still not sure if anyone is. But we know there wasn't a single person who had all the answers about how the virus would spread, the damage it would do, and how we should handle what was happening in 2020. It was really hard on us, because generally speaking, we humans don't do well with uncertainty. In a time when we can Google just about anything, and answers are just a couple of clicks away, we seem to have lost the ability to sit with the unknown. We need answers and we need them now. This need became apparent during the pandemic, as people with absolutely no rational reason to think they had the answers started acting like they did. We had our opinions, our righteousness, and our arrogance. We were surrounded on social media and in conversations with people who could not—would not—own what they're not. This turned people into armchair experts, lunatics, and judgmental assholes. Would it not have been refreshing if the *non*-infectious disease medical experts in our lives said, "There is so much that's unknown at this time, and I'm hearing conflicting information as we learn more. I'm uncertain of who to trust, and it's scary, so I'm going to try my best to do what I believe is right for me and my family. I'm happy to share my reasoning, but I'm not the decider of what's right for everybody. I'm not a policy or medical expert, so I will consider what those people say. I'd ask that you respect my decisions, as I'll respect yours, even if what you do goes against what I believe. I'm sure you have your beliefs and reasons, too." I'd have fallen off my chair if someone had said that to me, and then probably listened intently to whatever else they had to say. At the very least, there would have been a lot less ranting, hatred, and foaming at the mouth.

Owning what we're not as a global population would have allowed us to keep an open mind and seek out information from those who were most qualified to guide us through. It has been a mess, but speaking for myself, owning that I don't have the answers allowed me to go with the flow a lot more, and not waste whatever precious energy I had left on arguments where everybody loses. As adults and parents, Jay and I had to make decisions about how our family should handle the pandemic without letting it drive us crazy. That approach has gotten us through it and maybe even made us better, as difficult as it has been.

Though it may seem counterintuitive, the byproduct of building confidence by owning what we're not is an increase in other people's trust in us, which is a bonus on top of the trust you build with yourself! When you can admit what's not your area of expertise, the people around you will notice your integrity. They'll believe the things you tell them and know that they can rely on you to speak the truth when it matters. Understanding that no one has everything figured out is a conclusion we should all come to when we reach adulthood.[16] We should be skeptical of people who insist they have all the answers, are experts in every subject, or who claim to be happy and successful all the time. People like that are either masking a whole lot of insecurity, have no self-awareness, or have narcissistic personality disorder. They don't own or communicate

---

[16] Better ask your teenagers now, while they still know everything!

the whole story. They won't share anything they think would make them look bad and are only aware of what needs fixing in other people. The finger never points inward. When you can't own what you're not, it's like you're giving someone a false picture-perfect product pitch, and you're doing it with your entire being. No one wants that, and it does horrible damage to you! People who buy a product want to hear the pros and the cons. They want to know what it can do for them and what it can't. They want to know what to expect. In the same way, the people we encounter in life want to know what they can expect of us.

But all of that is less important than this: knowing the pros and cons, knowing what to expect, knowing what you can count on and what you shouldn't from *yourself* builds trust. Every attempt at perfection will damage your confidence. Embracing your imperfections will build it. Kind of mind-blasting, right?

AN EXERCISE FOR OWNING WHAT YOU'RE NOT

When it comes to owning what we're not, some things are much easier to accept about ourselves than others. If you're struggling with this in certain areas, you're not alone. I've found it's easier to get to the other side of this challenge by asking myself three questions: Is it true, does it matter, and what do I want to do with it right now?

Let's take a couple of the examples I've given so far. I'm not tall, and I have no trouble accepting the fact that I'm not tall. I have, however, often struggled with the fact that I'm not patient. So here's how this might work, using those two things I'm not as examples:

Step 1: Ask yourself, "Is it true?"

I'm five feet two on a good day, so based in fact, I'm not tall. I might be taller than a few people, but it's pretty easy to accept this as fact. By asking myself whether the statement, "I'm not a patient person," is also true, I can consider whether it's a fact, a matter of perception, or just a random thought. I can figure out whether I'm operating from an idea that was only true once or under certain circumstances, or if there is a pattern, theme, or consistency. If it's not consistently true, I let it go. In this case, not being a patient person is a matter of perception, but it has been consistent enough, and I have lots of evidence of it in my life, so it feels like a truth to me.

If I can answer that with a yes, I move on to the next question. If the answer is no, then I let it go! For example, if someone were to tell me that I'm a flaky person, I'd ask myself, "Is it true?" Yes, I've flaked on some things and some people at some points in my life. But on the whole, I'm somebody you can count on. The answer to "Is it true?" in this case would be no, so I'd move on with my life.

Step 2: Ask yourself, "Does it matter?"

Does not being tall matter to me? Well, for a time in my early teenage years where I thought being a model was the key to happiness, it mattered far too much. But outside of those painful months (and the challenge of grabbing things off of tall shelves) it has never impacted my life. Since not being tall doesn't matter, I let it go. Does being impatient matter? It affects my relationships, parenting, my purpose, goals, connections with other people, and my overall happiness. So yeah, it matters. It can impact the quality of my communication, which in turn can harm my professional credibility and ability to help those I want to serve. If being impatient didn't matter one way or the other, I'd let it go; but because it does, I move on to the third question.

Step 3: Ask yourself, "What do I want to do with it right now?"

Is it something I want to work on? Do I want to focus on growing or developing that specific skill? Do I want to try to improve myself in that area? Can I leverage someone or something else to support me? Or do I want to delegate the tasks I don't have patience for to someone else and give myself space to focus on my strengths? By sorting through these kinds of considerations, we can come to sensible conclusions about how we want to handle them rather than staying in beat-up mode. Instead of letting my impatience be a major character flaw I'm ashamed of, I own it. Owning it allows me to do something productive about it. We can narrow down the areas in life where we'd like to grow most. Then we can either do that work or move on from worrying about it. This process has helped me get comfortable with owning the many things I'm not. I'm not patient, and at this point, that's OK with me. It's a skill I've worked on, discussed in therapy, and learned to embrace. I'll always need to work on it, but I've also discovered many ways to leverage others and communicate so it doesn't become a major roadblock for me. I've also discovered several strengths associated with it, like quick decision-making, a willingness to take risks, and efficiency. Knowing this allows me to be confident about it, even though it's a clear example to anyone who's ever been in a relationship with me, or worked with me, that I'm far from perfect.

The conclusions we come to in terms of owning what we're not will always be personal and unique to us. Not being tall might matter greatly to you, and that's OK. The life you want to live will require different strengths than mine. As always, you're the decider here. Just keep in mind that the things that, on the surface, may feel like they're not working are just as important to confidence-building as the things in your life that are. Those aspects of yourself that feel less than ideal all have their place and provide balance. As much as it might seem embarrassing or shameful to acknowledge it, most of us figure out our purpose, our mission in life, and our value to others through pain and difficulty. And letting go of what's not meant for you creates time and space to home in on what is. As is true in so much of life, it helps to deal with things head on.

EMBRACING IT ALL

Once you're able to tackle the steps of knowing who you are and owning what you're not, you get to choose to embrace all of it. All of *you*. As we'll talk about in chapter nine, connecting with our confidence is a choice. You don't have to do it. You can go your entire life feeling insecure, as far too many people do, but that will put you at a disadvantage. It will put up walls between you and everything you want. Choosing to embrace your entire self, even the parts you don't like, is part of advocating for the most confident version of you. This is all about the lens through which we view ourselves. I don't just accept that I'm not patient. I embrace it because it's an important part of who I am. If I were patient, I'm not sure who I'd be, but I do know my life and career would be very different. And if I hadn't learned to embrace my impatience, I would've never done the work to develop that skill or leveraged others to help me. My goal in developing myself was not to become a patient person. That's not going to happen for me. My goal was to prevent it from becoming a roadblock in my life and career. But owning it allowed me to do something about it, which prevented me from becoming an asshole. And embracing it supported me in finding the good, the opportunity, within my "flaw."

The process of building confidence by working through knowing who you are, owning who you're not, and embracing all of it is an ongoing journey. You won't automatically feel like you're able to do it in every moment. It's a choice you get to continually make based on where you are in life, the information you're currently working with, and the circumstances unfolding around you. You get to reassess things and change your mind when necessary. At the end of the day, when you're able to connect with your confidence, you'll be working from the fundamental belief that you're going to be OK no matter what.

In part one of this book, we explored the topic of confidence through the lens of the female experience. We've talked about what confidence is, what it isn't, and why the definition matters. We've talked about the confidence gap and its impact on our lives. We've gone through general tips for how we can use our definition of confidence to begin the process of building our own. Next, we're going to zero in on five specific things that derail our confidence and the antidotes we can use to build real, sustainable, bring-it-on-because-I-have-important-shit-to-do confidence. In a world of experts telling you to *be* confident, I'm going to share *how* you actually build it.

ACTIVITY RECAP

Is it true, does it matter, and what do I want to do with it right now?

STEP 1: Ask yourself if the statement you can't accept is true. If so, move on to the next question. If not, let it go.

STEP 2: Ask yourself, "Does it matter?" If so, move on to the next question. If not, let it go.

STEP 3: Ask yourself, "What do I want to do with it right now?" and figure out a solution that will work for you at this time.

See how this exercise works for you!

PART 3

FIVE CONFIDENCE DERAILERS AND THEIR ANTIDOTES, THE CONFIDENCE BUILDERS

CHAPTER 6

Perfectionism and Failure

"There's no need to be perfect to inspire others.
Let people get inspired by how you
deal with your imperfections."

—Ziad K. Abdelnour

I DON'T KNOW ABOUT YOU, but I'm fed up with people telling women to be confident and yet never sharing *how*. Or, even worse, telling us that if we buy this product, invest in this course, or spend an outrageous amount of money on some quick fix, we'll be confident—and when we do, the feeling is only temporary, or it's contingent on our continuing to buy more. There will be none of that here. It ends now. I'm going to share five specific things that could be (and probably are) derailing your confidence, and I'm also going to share effective antidotes for not only disarming them, but building, keeping, and growing your confidence in the long term.

CONFIDENCE DERAILER	CONFIDENCE BUILDER
Perfectionism	Failure
Head Trash	Giving Grace on the Journey
Overthinking	Action
Comparison and Judgment	Choosing Confidence
Seeking Confidence Externally	Building Confidence Internally

I use the word "derailer" because each of these problems is separating you from your trust in yourself. They will chip away at, damage, and destroy your confidence if you let them. It might surprise you to see that the derailers are not external slights or attacks from other people. These derailers are habits we internalize as a result of the false and mixed messages we've received our whole lives. Essentially, we do them to ourselves. The five confidence builders can all be beneficial and will work in any scenario, but I've paired each with the derailer it directly corresponds to and combats most effectively.

I've found that in both my personal and professional life, if you start with tools to build confidence, but aren't aware or mindful of what derails it in the first place, you'll end up frustrated and disappointed, feeling like you're on the confidence hamster wheel. You'll be working, running, and believing you're moving forward toward confidence, but not actually getting anywhere. You might end up thinking, "I must be doing something wrong. Why isn't this working for me?" So while I will indeed share what will build your confidence, I first have to make sure you're aware of what's chipping away at it. It's hard to protect yourself from something if you don't know what it is, and these confidence derailers are doing major damage, specifically to women.

I'll begin with the confidence derailer that oh-so-many of us know all too well, and the one I personally struggle with the most: perfectionism. Every single time I speak on the topic of confidence and mention perfectionism, the vast majority of women in the audience start nodding their heads. If you're type A, a professional who stresses over delivering error-free work, a mom who loses sleep over burnt cookies, or someone who believes some of your value is rooted in how you look, you've probably battled with perfectionism. Let's talk about its antidote so you can not only counteract this particular poison, but also know the habits that will truly build your confidence in the face of it.

PERFECTIONISM IS THE ENEMY OF CONFIDENCE

Read that again. Perfectionism is the *enemy* of confidence.[17] It's not ever going to be confidence-building to aim for perfection. It's not even confidence-adjacent. It's the confidence nemesis. The

---

[17] If you want more on this, I'd highly recommend The Confidence Code by Katty Kay & Claire Shipman. It was here that I first heard this wisdom, and I'm forever grateful for it. They also have a version of the book for girls!

opponent. The "bad guy." You will *never* arrive at confidence via the perfectionism highway. Think of perfectionism as your dream home on the outside but down to the studs on the inside. There's faulty wiring, bad pipes, the joists need replacing, and the goddamn heat won't work. It's a facade. A big fat lie. It looks good to everyone else but is awful to live in.

Perfectionism, for so many women, is the belief that we're supposed to *do* it all, *have* it all, *be* it all, and look good while doing it. It's an unrealistic way to live because (#SpoilerAlert) nobody is perfect, yet we apply this impossible standard to ourselves on a regular basis. The extent to which we torture ourselves over this unattainable goal is a little nuts.[18]

In my house, we've replaced the saying, "practice makes perfect" with "practice makes *progress*" because I want to do everything in my power to make sure JJ knows that there's nothing she can do to create perfection. I say it for myself, too, because I spent a large part of my life thinking if I could just do it all, then I'd prove myself worthy, and having it all would be the reward. I've tried it, and it doesn't work. I tell JJ I love her "all the time" as a reminder that she doesn't have to earn my love. Then we'll have a little fun with it. I'll ask her, "Even when I'm traveling for work?"

Yes.

"Even when you make a mistake?"

---

[18] I say this with love!

Yes.

"Even if I'm feeling frustrated?"

Yes.

"Even when I'm pooping in the bathroom?"

Yes.

(She's eight and poop jokes are all the rage.)

My goal is for her to know that she doesn't have to perform or prove herself to be worthy of love. She just is.

The reality is, we often connect most deeply with other people through our imperfections. We bond with our friends, partners, and clients by commiserating about our challenges and our pain. It opens up space for the level of intimate connection we seek with others, but none of that can happen when there's no realness, transparency, or vulnerability. We can actually drive people away when we broadcast perfection as our standard because they see that we're unwilling to make space in our lives for anything less, and that's daunting. We're *all* going through something all the time. As a recovering perfectionist myself, I don't trust people, organizations, or cultures that are always positive because it's not real. There's something being glossed over or hidden beneath the surface. So if confidence is about trust, perfectionism ultimately works against us. It keeps us from fostering deep connections with the very people who might actually be able to tolerate, support, forgive, and encourage us when we (*gasp!*) display our humanity by making a mistake. It also keeps us from fostering any type of connection with our*selves*.

Many of us have become perfectionists in the first place in an attempt to avoid pain. We think that if we get everything right, we'll avoid criticism and people will love and admire us. We think if we perform well enough and work hard enough, we'll get the recognition, lifestyle, and success we deserve. We believe that if we look good enough and manipulate ourselves just right, we'll attract the love and acceptance we crave and never have to experience heartbreak. We imagine if we just do and say everything right as parents, our kids will lead happy and fulfilling lives free of pain. In truth, none of us will ever completely avoid pain in life and, ironically enough, by making this desperate attempt to avoid it, we create more. We avoid taking bold risks for fear that someone might see us fail. We get into and stay in all kinds of relationships that don't serve us because we question whether we're good enough. On top of that, we're crushed when we do fall short of expectations because we think it proves there's something fundamentally wrong with who we are. And like other marginalized groups in society, women feel the need to perform at our maximum potential at all times because it feels like someone is always watching, and if we drop the ball even once, it'll shatter at our feet. We feel the need to do more so we can be valued, and although there's truth behind that, we'll never be able to eradicate sexism by striving to rise to society's unrealistic demands. Likewise, we'll never achieve confidence through perfectionism.

When we step back and think about it, we can all see that there are consequences for the effort and energy we put into trying to make ourselves perfect, and they're exhausting. There's avoiding risk, imposter syndrome, the fear of being exposed, anxiety, depression, stress, lack of sleep, toxic relationships, the inability to learn from our mistakes, and more. That's what perfectionism is costing you. Is it worth the price? At the end of the day you have to ask yourself what you want and how badly you want it. You want amazing, healthy relationships? You want a phenomenal working environment? You want to be confident? Well, you can't have any of those things and hold onto perfectionism at the same time. The two cannot coexist, so you're going to have to choose. Are you willing to let go of what you *know* isn't going to work and risk what you fear *might* not end up working? Only you can answer this, but I assume you wouldn't choose to suffer more than you have to on purpose.

Sometimes, people will tell me that they know they have high expectations of themselves or others, but that this works for them. If it's working for you, that's awesome, and I can relate. But if it's perfectionism at play, you're doing damage to your confidence. What about being growth-oriented instead? That's an amazing quality and not at all the same as perfectionism. Confident people are growth-oriented, but trust themselves as they're growing. Perfectionists tend to feel nothing is ever good enough and that they need to achieve perfection before they'll feel confident. See the difference? So, if perfectionism is the enemy of confidence and the biggest derailer for most women, how do we counteract it?

THE ANTIDOTE TO PERFECTIONISM IS FAILURE

Yes, you read that right. Failure. Before you break into a cold sweat, I'm not suggesting that you go out and purposefully fail at everything. But you will need to make mistakes, feel pain, put yourself out there, and get rejected in order to build your confidence. You'll probably need to fail in big ways, small ways, private ways, and public ways. Fail over and over and over again on a regular basis for the rest of your life. That's the answer.

I know what you're thinking: "Nicole, that's the craziest bullshit I've ever heard!" Or maybe you don't curse as much in your head as I do and are just thinking "I *hate* failure." Of course you do. We all do! I feel the same way about failure that I do about working out. It sucks while I'm doing it, but I make myself do it anyway. I know there are people who enjoy exercising, and if you do, God bless you; but I do it for the growth, strength, and health only. Enjoyment has never been a part of it for me and is not a requirement for doing it. It'll never be comfortable or fun, and I'll never love it. When we exercise, we tear up our muscles, and they become stronger as they heal. The same is true of failure. Rather than learning to love it, we must learn to *accept* it as a necessary part of our growth and betterment as humans.

We can learn to accept failure by creating a more empowered, more productive interpretation of our mistakes, missteps, and imperfections. As women, we tend to personalize our failures at a far greater level than our male counterparts do. We view them as a reflection of our overall worth and value as human beings. A man might do a bad job on a presentation and think, "Damn, I didn't plan well enough or do a good enough job of explaining my point." He might even think he did a great job when he didn't. As women, we'd be more likely to let a bad presentation consume us and end up exaggerating to the point of thinking, "I suck as a leader. My communication skills are awful," or "I don't know what I'm doing and now everyone knows." We need to shift our mindset by understanding that, objectively speaking, "failure" is a *neutral event,* and we're the ones who assign meaning to it. My coach, Lisa, says we're "meaning-making machines." Logically, we can see this is true, because something you see as an insurmountable failure could seem easy to overcome by someone else. And something that seems like no big deal to you could feel incredibly damaging to another. For example, I know someone who started their business year at a deficit of almost a quarter of a million dollars. They lost $250k before the year had even started and were slightly uncomfortable, while for most of us, that level of debt would be *devastating.* Another example is when we get our heart broken for the first time as teenagers. An adult might look at that and go, "No big deal. You'll get over it. You were too young for it to work. It wasn't going to last, anyway. You'll find the right person eventually. " And while that might make sense to us, having your heart broken for the first time is *soul-crushing* to a teenager. We all go through pain in life, and it will never not suck when you're going through it, but it helps to realize our failure serves a purpose and is mostly temporary—or, at the very least, evolving.

If we think back and look at the most life-altering events that completely changed the trajectory of our lives for the better, chances are most of them come as a result of overcoming a failure or living through some kind of pain. It can be the hard times, the transitions, and the moments when we put our foot down and decide, "I can't do this anymore," or "I don't want to live like this," that change everything for us. A lot of us interpret our negative emotions during these experiences as a sign that there's something wrong with us.

Let's take the expression "Quitting is for losers" and run it through the perfectionist derailer, followed by our confidence builder. A perfectionist doesn't give up because they must get it right, thereby implying that all you need is to *do better*, or *do more*, and it'll all work out. Yes, the expression is meant to be motivating, but really, quitting can be for winners if it leads to better mental, emotional, and physical health. Quitting an abusive relationship? *Winner*. Walking away from a job where your work isn't valued? That's a win, too. Giving up on a goal that was never your own and you were just doing it to please someone else? Win! But in order to win in all of those examples, you'd need to "give up," let go, admit defeat, or possibly experience failure. You'd also probably be better served if you chose to look at those events as opportunities, gifts, or lessons. Sure, life would be easy if you met the person of your dreams in your first crush, started the career of your dreams right out of college, only ever achieved the goals that got you exactly where you wanted, and everything was perfect all the time. But that's not an available option for any of us—and frankly, without the lows, we wouldn't appreciate the highs.

Letting go of perfectionism? Biggest win of them all! Consider for a minute if you were to quit on the expectation of doing, looking, and being perfect. Wouldn't that free you up to listen to your inner knowing, live your life more authentically, and spend more time doing what actually matters to you? Ultimately, what I'm saying is that we have the opportunity to change our interpretation of our life events to create a more empowering, productive perception that honors our inherent worth. And since we're the ones making up what our failures, mistakes, and pain mean anyway, we might as well make up a meaning that works for us.

One note on perfectionism and failure that's specific to women: I've noticed women's *fear* of failure is often more debilitating than any actual failure. We tend to focus on the worst possible outcome or think of the worst-case scenario, especially when taking a risk. Perfectionism holds us back from even trying because we know subconsciously that we won't be perfect, and we let the fear of the unknown or that worst-case, life-destroying failure prevent us from doing anything. I know not only from personal experience, but in my experience working with and coaching hundreds of women, that the worst-case scenario almost never happens. Hardly anything turns out as badly as we think it will, but we get stuck imagining our suffering as if it's a foregone conclusion. A better opportunity is to think about all the worst things that could happen and ask, "How would I handle that?" Confidence isn't about not facing or having any challenges. Confidence is when you trust that you can get through the challenges. If you're going to ask yourself about the worst that could happen, make sure you also ask, "What's the *best* thing that could happen?" and marinate on that just as much while trying to predict the future. By doing so, we view the whole picture of possible outcomes of the risks we take rather than being blinded by incomplete information. And, we actually better prepare ourselves, because we're thinking about how we'll face and overcome any failures, while simultaneously expecting that good things will happen! (We'll explore this in more depth when I talk about overthinking in chapter eight.)

PROCESSING OUR FAILURES FROM A NEUTRAL PERSPECTIVE

So, how do we reframe our failures into something that works for us? How do we begin to interact with the possibility of failure in a different way? How in God's name do we begin to think of and leverage failure as a confidence *builder*? The answer is practice. Lots of practice, the same way you get good at just about anything.

I'm going to share a tactic that I use to coach myself and pretty much every person I work with. I developed it after picking it up from my own coach, Lisa, and it has now become my go-to every time I'm dealing with my personal and professional mistakes.

Step 1: Think about the situation, event, feeling, or freak-out you find yourself in, and ask the question: "What are the facts?"

Think *only* about the objective facts related to the situation and write them down. To give you an example, I launched an online course on November 2, 2020, the same day of a rather well-known presidential election. (Maybe you remember it?) I got exactly two people registered for my course in the first week, one of them being my uber supportive and thoughtful husband. Let's just say this was not quite the result I'd anticipated. It was worse than all the worst-case scenarios I'd imagined. I'd invested close to $20k to create and market the course, had spent hours upon hours promoting it on social media, and felt great about what I'd created. My big goal was to sell 300 courses, and while I didn't anticipate it happening in the first week, I was shocked that only one person signed up who wasn't someone I was sleeping with. Feelings of failure, embarrassment, fear, and doubt were circling my brain like rabid vultures. I knew if I didn't get a hold of myself and work through them, they would consume me. I also had the advantage of having just built a confidence course, so I ended up taking my own course to deal with it. So, what were the facts? The facts were that I'd never launched an online course before. It was my first time, so the entire thing was new to me. I had no data to rely on, no experience in that space, and I didn't do much research before creating it. I released the course on 11/2/20, which was the same day as an election, which in a historic turn of events wasn't called until several days later. The fact is that two people registered in the first week, and although I'd set an initial goal of selling 300 courses, I sold 68 courses in the first year. Those are some examples of the facts.

Step 2: Ask yourself, "What am I making up about the facts?"

What have I decided that the facts mean, what is the story I'm telling myself, or what is my interpretation of the event or situation? In my example, I was making up that I'd failed miserably, nobody saw value in the work I do, I'd made a bad investment, and I was a horrible business owner. The story I was telling myself was that I'd be humiliated if anyone found out how severely short of my goal I'd fallen. That I should have known better because launching on the same day as a major election was plain stupid. "What kind of idiot does that?!?" I was telling myself that people didn't like me, my work, or anything I had to say. *They'll all think I'm a hack and the naysayers were right.* I could go on for days, despite the *fact* that outside of that online course, I was still running a six-figure business and had achieved some other major successes that year. We could *all* go on for days making up all sorts of terrible things about ourselves. That doesn't mean any of them are true. Separating the facts from what you're making up about the facts can help you recognize the difference between reality and the story you're telling yourself, which is incredibly powerful as we transition into the next step.

Step 3: Ask, "What's a different, more productive, more empowered way of seeing this?"

This question is a game-changer because it reminds you that you are the one in control of your perception, and you have a choice to see things in a completely different way! You literally get to choose between beating yourself up or empowering yourself. This, by the way, is not the same as lying to yourself. I'm not suggesting you make up whatever feels good. I'm suggesting you interpret the facts in a way that actually serves you. Sometimes it helps to ask someone you trust how they see it, like a coach, mentor, friend, or partner. In my example, I could also have said any of the following to myself:

It was the first time I launched an online course. Of course I was going to make mistakes and not get it all right. I'd never expect anyone to crush something the first time they did it. I learned a ton from the experience and figured out many things I won't do again and some things I would do exactly the same. Sixty-eight people did register for and take the course, so not only did I cover the investment I'd made of money, time, and energy in creating it, but I actually made a small profit. The people who participated in the course got to experience it and came out with a greater understanding of confidence. I got to interact with them, get their feedback, and hear their amazing stories. If someone thinks I'm a hack because one launch didn't go as planned, that's a them problem, not a me problem. This particular risk didn't pay off the way I'd hoped, but it did pay off in many other ways. If someone finds joy in my mistake and wants to gossip about it, that's okay. I love when assholes make themselves known, as it makes it easier for me to sort them out of my life.

The list of more productive, more empowering things I could be telling myself goes on and on. And frankly, while I'm just telling myself that better version of the facts, it actually feels truer and more grounded in fact than the other story I made up. From this experience, I also discovered that online courses aren't what I want to be doing with my time. It ended up distracting me from other things I was more passionate about. None of these benefits are exaggerations. They're just a different perspective of the same failure, but this new perspective will build my confidence, while the other won't.

Step 4: Ask yourself, "What's next?"

How do you get into action from here? The importance of this question will become clear in chapter eight, but now that you've chosen a more productive and empowered interpretation of your failure, mistake, pain, or fear, what do you want to do about it? What's the next best thing you can do? What action will get you closer to what matters to you? What's something you can do that will make you feel proud? If you trusted yourself, what would you do next? I could laundry-list all the things that came after my foray into selling online courses, but you're literally holding one of them in your hands. This book is what I did next. I didn't start writing it immediately, but I did start putting one foot in front of the other, and those action steps are what got me here. That failure led me to this bucket-list moment and increased my confidence so much that I literally wrote a book about it.

The next time you're stuck in the muck, give this exercise a try! It has been life- changing for me and so many women that I work with, as it is an opportunity to build the habit of seeing "failure" from a more productive, accurate, and empowered place. This exercise works for men, too, by the way; but I find it particularly impactful for women because we tend to internalize our failures, mistakes, hurt, and fear at a greater level than our male counterparts do. I'm generalizing here, but women tend to jump from "I failed" to "I am a failure" way too much, way too fast. We let our failures define us, but those experiences say nothing about our inherent value or worth as a human. Men tend to bounce back and get back into action faster, and they tend not to *avoid* taking risks as often because they don't walk into scenarios thinking, "The outcome of this is going to say everything about me." In my observation, men have certain areas where perfectionism plays out (i.e., success, income, provide, protect), but they don't hold themselves to the expectation of perfection in all aspects of their lives, so they don't put so much weight on every single decision. We don't have to, either. We can fail. We can see failure as something we did, not something we are.

We can also pick ourselves up, dust ourselves off, and get back into action toward what matters. We call that failing forward. The only real failure is to stop trying.

WHAT WILL BE, WILL BE

Failure will build your confidence and lead you to greater success if you let it. If you allow it. If you *choose* it. Failure builds confidence because it builds trust in yourself. You begin to have confidence that you can survive hardship and come out the other side better and stronger, having learned something. You collect evidence that you can overcome your failures, mistakes, fear and pain. The next time you face a tough challenge, risk, or big decision, you'll know from experience that you can make it through no matter what, and that you'll come out the other side better, if you choose to. I'm willing to take uncomfortable risks and fail at a higher rate than most people. Why? Because I know in my heart of hearts that it'll all work out one way or another. And as Jay often tells me, "What's the alternative? Give up?" No thank you. I will not be giving up on my goals, passions, and dreams. What will be will be. There's no sense in robbing ourselves of opportunities to do amazing things for fear of outcomes we can't possibly predict. You deserve better.

So there you have it, friends! Your first confidence derailer is perfection, and its antidote is the most surprising confidence builder of them all: failure. This leads us to our next derailer, because perfectionism is an extra special brand of destruction. It not only sets us up for unachievable goals; it's a one-two punch that also has us beating ourselves up about it. I call this internal dialogue head trash, and it's crushing our confidence.

ACTIVITY RECAP

An Exercise for Processing Failure

STEP 1: Think about the situation and ask yourself, "What are the facts?"

STEP 2: Ask yourself, "What am I making up about the facts?"

STEP 3: Ask, "What's a different, more productive, more empowered way of seeing this?" Reframe your perception to align with that vision.

STEP 4: Ask yourself, "What's next?" so you can get into action.

How did this exercise work for you?[19]

---

[19] This activity is based on content originally created by Byron Katie. For a deeper dive, visit her website at www.thework.org.

CHAPTER 7

Head Trash and Giving Grace on the Journey

"You spend most of your life inside your head.
Make it a nice place to be."

—Unknown

I COACH A LOT OF INCREDIBLE WOMEN, and it always surprises me to hear their self-talk is just nasty in spite of everything they're accomplishing. An entrepreneur running her own six-figure business while raising two young children used to tell me, "I need to get my shit together." This blew my mind. She hadn't gotten a full night's sleep in over eight months, was the primary breadwinner for her family at the time, and was also smack dab in the middle of building her own house. She managed a team, was engaged in her kids' lives, cared about her community, and was increasing her revenue year after year. This woman had her shit, and everyone else's shit, together. Yet, that's what she believed about herself.

"If someone you loved was working as hard as you are while raising two young kids and building a house, would you tell them they needed to get their shit together?" I asked.

"No, never," she answered.

"Then why do you feel like it's okay to say that to *yourself*?"

This is head trash. It's the things we say *to* ourselves, *about* ourselves, that are never kind and rarely true. It's a cruel internal dialogue that is also referred to as the inner critic, superego, or negative thoughts. I know we all know what it's like to hear it. "I'm such an idiot. What the fuck is wrong with me? I'm so lazy. I'm ugly, fat, have too much *this*, not enough *that*. I'm not good enough. I'm a failure. What if someone notices…" We say awful things in our own mind—things we would never say out loud to anyone we love. Would you ever say what you say to yourself to your partner, best friend, sister, or child? I think (and hope) not. A lot of women tell me they can't stop their head trash, but I know that's not true. They stop themselves from being unkind toward the people they love all the time.

We can't eliminate our negative thoughts altogether, but we can work to notice them faster and put a process in place that replaces them with kinder, gentler, more productive thoughts. I've seen my clients skyrocket their performance, revenue, and success thanks to this one impactful change in mindset. Frankly, you'd be hard-pressed to find a coach, expert, athlete, or successful professional that would tell you that mindset doesn't matter. I'd go as far as to say that everything in your life begins with your mindset. It's *that* important. Mindset and manifesting are all the rage right now, and just like confidence, I see a lot of misconceptions, misrepresentations, and general crap about what those words actually mean. Our mindset is the set of beliefs that shapes the way we make sense of our world and ourselves. It creates our perception and interpretation of everything, which of course influences how we feel, think, and act. Manifestation is when you create or bring forth something through your beliefs and the laws of attraction that shows up in a tangible way. I think of it as, "If you believe it, it will come."

OK, so why am I defining mindset and manifestation? Because those thoughts in your head create your reality. And if your thoughts are consumed by head trash, you're going to create patterns, themes, and results in your life that don't serve you and keep you from what you really want. In this chapter, we're going to talk about head trash and how giving ourselves grace along the journey enables us to rebuild our confidence.

WHAT MY ACTUAL TRASH TAUGHT ME

I've learned a lot about head trash from my actual trash. Seriously. My family moved from California to Massachusetts back in 2017 after Jay had been offered an amazing career opportunity on the East Coast. Being that I can do my work as a speaker and coach from anywhere, the decision for him to take it was a no-brainer. In the space of two and a half months, we sold our house in California, bought a house on the East Coast, packed up all our stuff and our three-year-old at the time, and moved. And because Jay needed to start his new role quickly, I took on most of the logistics.

We didn't have a lot of time to research the town we were moving to, and Jay hadn't even seen the house we bought until he did the final inspection. Let's just say this period in our lives was a little chaotic and a lot stressful. One of the surprises we discovered after we'd arrived in our new town was that it didn't provide trash service. Residents don't leave their bins out on the curb every week for someone to come and collect. Nobody comes to pick up your waste and dispose of it for you there. We had to take all of our trash, recycling, and compost, pack it in the trunk of my car, and take it to a place called the "transfer station," which is a nice way of saying "the dump."

Managing this task became my job. Please note: Jay and I divvy up chores and household responsibilities, so before you start feeling sorry for me or get riled up that I'm expected to handle all household responsibilities, know that he does 100 percent of the grocery shopping and cooking in our house. Handling the trash every week was an easy yes for me. And in doing this, I learned three valuable insights into how head trash is similar to real trash.

Lesson 1: I'm not the only person who contributes to my trash.

In the case of the waste I dropped off at the transfer station, many people were involved in adding to it. There were daily contributions from Jay and JJ, trash from friends and family members when they came to visit, and the random debris the wind blew into our yard. Dinner parties with friends, colleagues, or clients would quickly double the load. The more people that were around, the higher the pile grew. Head trash works the same way. Not all, in fact probably not most, of it is ours alone. Things your parents and family said to or around you, whether they had good intentions for saying them or not, have contributed to your head trash. You've picked it up from friends, exes, bosses, coworkers, bullies, influencers, and strangers on social media. Everywhere you turn, there's the possibility that someone might add to your load. When your head trash talks to you, it's not just your voice alone that you're hearing. It's worth asking yourself where all those dirty rags and shards of glass are coming from. It's worth asking whose voice it is and whether it's worth listening to.

Lesson 2: Regardless of how much or how many other people contributed to my trash, it was still my job to sort, sift, and discard it.

During that time in my life, I had to separate the trash, recycling, and compost waste and make sure to take them to the right places at the transfer station. Sometimes, after parties, I'd realize that guests threw cans in with the regular trash and had to move them over to recycling. Food waste would pile up with the garbage, so we bought a little can for the things we could compost. This was my chore to get done and no one was going to do it for me. To get everything in its proper place, I had to dig in, get my hands dirty, sort, sift, and discard appropriately. Just like head trash. You can sort through your negative thoughts and decide what to do with them and where they belong. There are thoughts in your head that you might choose to recycle, meaning they can be reused in another way or brought back for another purpose. There are thoughts that should be composted because they can be used for your own growth and betterment. And there are *definitely* thoughts that are straight trash and should be tossed out for good, never to be seen or thought of again. It will always be your job to sort, sift, and discard your head trash, no matter how many people have added to it. It's your life, your mind, and your confidence; and therefore, the buck stops with you. Since I know most of you haven't had to be your own trash collectors and disposers, let me give you some examples. People have often directly told me or alluded to the idea that I am too driven and ambitious (for a woman). Over time, I began to recognize that I could recycle this thought in my head into something positive and motivating. Yes, I am driven and ambitious! Yes, I want to achieve goals, make a difference, and create the life I want. *Thank you* for recognizing and reminding me that I already have that inside me and I can use it to create professional success. The people saying it to me might have thought these were bad traits, but I don't. And my belief about myself is what matters, so I'm going to use that as fuel, thank you very much! My drive and ambition have propelled me to accomplish a great deal professionally. I didn't need to throw that away; I just needed to repurpose it. I've also heard, mostly from bullies and ex-boyfriends, that I'm loud and opinionated. That was obviously not meant as a compliment, but in the spirit of composting, how do I turn it into valuable fertilizer that enriches and helps me grow? Well, I started a podcast, like any loud and opinionated person does. And lastly, the amount of head trash I've had about my body could fill an entire transfer station on its own, but I've decided every negative thought about my body is trash and needs to be tossed out completely. It doesn't belong in my home, and I need to keep throwing it in the trash every time I see it. Your specific head trash will be different, but you can handle it the same way. You are the decider of where it belongs and what you want to do with it.

Lesson 3: The sorting, sifting, and discarding process becomes significantly more urgent and important when it's hot out.

During the humid summer months, our trash was *disgusting*. I'm talking mold, maggots, and a stench that would make a skunk gag. I would hold my breath while handling it wearing full gloves, laying out towels in my trunk before reluctantly loading it into my car for the journey to the transfer station. I had to do drop-offs more fre-quently than I did in the winter to keep the smell from becoming unbearable and so that my job didn't become even more revolting. The same goes for head trash when things "get hot" in our lives. When you're stressed, overwhelmed, in pain, or feeling exhausted, that's when you need to sort, sift, and discard more frequently to keep things from getting disgusting in your mind.[20]

To put this more directly, you are not a trash can. It is not your job to store your head trash. You are a temple, a home, and a frickin' miracle. The garbage wasn't there when you were born and you shouldn't allow it to contaminate the sacred space of your mind. There's a quote I love that says, "We can't prevent a bird from flying over our heads, but we can prevent it from building a nest in our hair." Similarly, we can't prevent negative thoughts from flying into our brains, but we can certainly stop them from taking up residence there and making themselves at home. This is challenging, but not as challenging as the alternative. Feeling like shit all the time because we're harsh toward ourselves is a cruel punishment I wouldn't even wish on my enemies. We're so quick to process those unkind words as incontrovertible truth, but poisonous words intended to hurt are almost always skewed exaggerations of reality. It's time to take out your trash.

---

[20] #NoMoreMindMaggots

THE ANTIDOTE TO HEAD TRASH IS GIVING
YOURSELF GRACE ON YOUR JOURNEY

To keep head trash from derailing our confidence, we have to learn the skill of giving ourselves grace on the journey. That "on the journey" part is important because it reminds us that confidence-building is a lifelong process. Like regular trash, head trash requires constant attention and clean-up. No one ever lands in a place of confidence, plants a flag, and gets to say, "That's it! I'm done! I'm confident forever!" There's no final destination for our inner work, and we get to embrace that. And because confidence-building is a journey, it's imperative that we be kind to and encourage ourselves along the way. By acknowledging our growth when it happens, we acknowledge how far our efforts have brought us. If we're to reach our full potential in spite of life's challenges, we *must* be somebody that we love first and foremost; therefore we must speak to ourselves in the same way we would a loved one. We, as much as anyone in our lives, deserve our own kindness.

What I'm ultimately talking about is replacing your head trash with gentler, more productive, more empowered messages that will inspire you to move through life with resilience. I have a two-part process I use to help me do this, and just like everything, it gets easier with practice.

Step 1: Name your negative or disempowered thought.

Listen to what you're telling yourself and ask whether you'd say it to a loved one. Would you say something like, "You'll never achieve your goal and aren't worthy of your dream life," to your soulmate or best friend? Of course not. Therefore, that's not your inner knowing, fact, or honest truth. Your inner knowing and the honest truth can absolutely be something you don't want to hear. The distinction to keep in mind is how the message is being said. Head trash is mean. It's basically you bullying yourself. Your inner knowing or hard truth will speak to you from a place of love, caring, and wanting the best for you. As an example, your head trash may say, "You can't do any better. Who do you think you are? If you leave him you'll be lonely, sad, and pathetic forever." Your inner knowing or honest truth might say, "It's time to move on. You deserve better, and you've put up with too much already. Yes, it will be painful, but you know what you need to do and you'll be OK." Naming it is so important because it helps you distinguish head trash from inner knowing, and helps you identify it for what it is: bullying yourself.

Once you've recognized what it is, you can choose what you want to do with it. Rather than letting head trash camp out in your brain, you can opt to move on.

Step 2: Replace the thought with something you'd actually say to someone you love.

This reframing process is the essence of giving grace, and there are a number of ways to do it. You can deal with the specific thought directly, replacing something like, "I'm never going to hit my goal" with "I haven't achieved my goal yet, but I've come a long way, and forward momentum will get me there." If there's a recurring negative thought that pops up often for you, you can decide on a phrase in advance to pull out as a mantra whenever it's needed. You might say, "I am enough, just as I am," or "I am patient with myself and embrace any progress I make," or "I celebrate my uniqueness because it's what makes me special." When my head trash kicks up and I haven't prepared a well-crafted affirmation, I simply say to myself, "gentle, gentle, gentle" as a reminder to be as gentle with myself as I would with anyone I love. If this feels difficult or forced in the beginning, that's normal, but keep at it. Our brains build habits quickly, and if you practice this simple strategy, you'll trigger healthier thoughts when you begin to feel cracks in your confidence.

You might get stuck on a particular piece of head trash and think something like, "It's the truth, though! I *am* lazy! I *am* incompetent! I *am* a horrible business owner! How can I replace that? Denial won't help me move forward." Denial is never helpful, but neither is putting ourselves down while we're trying to make progress. In cases like these, think back to the exercise we covered while talking about failure in the last chapter. It can be just as useful when we're feeling stubborn and dead-set on vilifying ourselves. What are the facts? What are you making up about the facts? What's a different, more productive, more empowered way to see it? What's next? Because most of the time, you're making it all up anyway.

None of this is meant to push you toward toxic positivity. Not everything needs to feel good or make us happy all the time. I'm not suggesting we do any of this to put lipstick on a pig or avoid getting real with ourselves. A lot of the time, we feel like people can either choose to be kind or choose to be honest, but there's *always* a way to do both at the same time. This is about being gentle with ourselves, keeping in mind that we are all works in progress. It's about challenging ourselves to resist the temptation to beat ourselves up so we can move forward. You're going to make mistakes. You're going to disappoint yourself and others. Life is going to throw shit at you, whether you like it or not, so the best way to deal with this is to get into the practice of communicating—especially with yourself—from a place of love and grace.

Something I hear truly confident people say often is, "I'm not sure." They hit those moments, stages, and periods of uncertainty along their journey and settle into the gray area rather than needing the black or white. They don't need to know it all or tell themselves they know nothing. They *trust* themselves. They give themselves grace and simply admit, "I don't have that figured out yet," while owning that there's nothing wrong with it. This type of vulnerability shows strength. It's a path to freedom. When we respect that we're not done yet, that we have more to accomplish and always will, we're more likely to savor every step of our personal adventure rather than just the milestones.

RIPPLES BECOME WAVES

For a lot of the women I work with, it takes months or even years to build the skill of choosing more empowered and productive thoughts while talking to themselves. Practice makes progress, however, and that has allowed them to achieve big goals that seemed out of reach and feel better about themselves in the process. Their level of talent stayed the same. Their opportunities remained steady. The only thing that changed about their approach was how they saw themselves in it.

Remember my amazing client that I mentioned at the beginning of this chapter? Mrs. I-Need-To-Get-My-Shit-Together? Flash forward to now, as I'm writing this book, and she's on the road to earning four times the income she was making when we first met. She is crushing life. She was *always* crushing life, but the practice of giving herself grace was the single biggest factor of boosting her success. It helped her take risks and continue moving forward with the confidence that the only person standing in her way was herself. When she begins to see herself the way I see her, the way anyone who has the privilege to interact with her sees her, she will tear the roof off, break all the glass, and create the life her inner knowing believes is possible. It has been a great joy and incredible honor to watch her grow, and she's just getting started. So I urge you to ask yourself, how is your self-talk holding you back from what you want? How can small ripples of confidence grow into tidal waves for you, too?

The two confidence derailers we've discussed so far often rely on help from the next one we're about to cover while doing their dirty work. Let's talk about overthinking.

ACTIVITY RECAP

An Exercise for Replacing Head Trash
with Empowerment

STEP 1: Name your negative or disempowered thought. If it's head trash, move on to Step 2.

STEP 2: Replace the thought with something you'd actually say to someone you love.

The next time head trash pops up in your mind, try this activity for yourself!

CHAPTER 8

Overthinking and Action

"Thinking will not overcome fear,
but action will."

—W. CLEMENT STONE

I DOUBT I NEED TO EXPLAIN what I mean by overthinking, but for women it often shows up in wanting to feel "ready," wanting to feel 100 percent confident before getting into action, and wanting to think through every possible scenario in every possible way in our own minds. Overthinking and perfectionism feel closely related to me; perfectionism is the outward demonstration while overthinking is the internal one. But they share the same root problem, which is that we're not trusting ourselves. I see this play out a ton with new business owners. The early stages of being an entrepreneur are their own special brand of scary. In many cases it involves giving up or stepping away from a "safe" income. I've heard it explained as jumping out of an airplane and building a parachute on the way down, which feels pretty accurate. But the amount of women I witness who *want* to jump, but never do because they're too busy checking every piece of equipment and researching the physics of gravity and air resistance, would blast your mind. They end up stuck on the damn plane until they run out of fuel.

OVERTHINKING IS A WASTE OF OUR TIME

Them: "Hey, I have a great opportunity for you! It comes with more growth, money, and impact."

You: "Hold on, let me just overthink it."

Have you ever done this? Don't lie, you know you have. We *all* have. Women constantly limit our potential for professional growth by deselecting ourselves out of positions, promotions, and other opportunities. In most cases, we do this because we don't think we're ready—but what's really problematic here is how we define *ready*. I can't tell you how many women have told me they don't feel 100 percent ready, which is basically the equivalent of saying "I don't feel perfect." They're waiting for something that's impossible. The only way we can ever become completely ready for anything is by doing it and getting experience under our belts. We think far too much, far too hard, and for far too long. We feel like we need to know every-damn-thing and analyze every potential pitfall before we can get into action. That is preventing us from taking action, which you're about to find out is a huge confidence builder.

Generally speaking, men don't engage in Olympic-level mental gymnastics the way we do. They don't repeat conversations in their heads for hours on end and dissect every single word. They don't seem to worry about every possible outcome or to overanalyze every potential pitfall. They don't ruminate for days about something that happened a week ago. I'm sure a few of us would make the argument that men just don't think, but the point I'm trying to make here is that they're less likely to *over*think.

Colin Powell created a management theory that he used as a military general and statesman called "the 40-70 rule." When faced with a big decision, his rule of thumb was to make sure he had at least 40 percent, but no more than 70 percent, of the information he needed to make a sound choice. Think about that for a minute. No more than 70 percent of the information needed to make the decision—and these were big, tough, life-and-death decisions. He didn't want to make the mistake of taking uninformed action (hence, the no less than 40 percent), but he also didn't want to wait until it was too late to take meaningful action (which is why it's important not to go over 70 percent). If he got stuck worrying about collecting every possible piece of info, he'd never end up getting into action. He knew 100 percent ready wasn't a viable option.

There's a lesson here we can all learn. Thinking is not a problem. *Over*thinking is the problem because it leads to *in*action. Inaction leads to regret, and regret chips away at our confidence. If you talk to most successful people, or people in the later stages of their lives, they share that they regret the things they *didn't* do far more than the things they did. They regret the dreams they didn't chase, the risks they didn't take, and the conversations they didn't have. They regret not jumping. Overthinking has the potential to create the same regrets for you, too. When you're overthinking, you can't be in action. All those things you don't spend your time doing, and the opportunities you don't expose yourself to while doing all that extra thinking, will build and eat away at you over time.

DON'T THINK WOMEN OVERTHINK?

Hah! Let's consider, for example, the last time any of us went on a first date.

(I know. It's painful. Bear with me.)

I think back to my first date with my now-husband Jay and thank my lucky stars that he wasn't able to observe, experience, or witness the overthinking that happened on my end. If he had, I'm not so sure there ever would have been a second date. And this is with someone who clearly was into me, given that he ended up marrying me. There were dates before I met him with other guys who weren't so into me, where the whole cycle of overthinking I went through was borderline psychotic. Jay actually *liked* me, and still I allowed my brain to become a cesspool of head trash that consumed too much of my time. Here's just a small example of my internal monologue after our first date:

Should I call him or wait for him to call me? How many days should I wait to get in touch? When we last texted he said this, and then I responded this, and then he didn't respond!! Did I offend him? Did I say something wrong? Should I text him again? Should I clarify what I meant? Should I ask a couple of people to read the texts and let me know what they think? Seven texts ago, I said I was going out of town; maybe he thinks he shouldn't bother me. Maybe he's just really busy. But I'm really busy, and I'd find a way to make the time to talk to him. Maybe he's not that interested. Let me think through every moment of the date and see if I did anything wrong. I knew I shouldn't have worn that dress. Do my texts sound as crazy as I'm feeling right now?!

And what was he thinking on the other end of this?

I had a nice time. I'll text her later.

In addition to holding us back from taking action, overthinking straight-up robs us of our joy. It limits us from being present in our experiences because we're so caught up in our heads, wondering "What does this mean?" We sit there projecting all sorts of ideas onto other people that may or may not have anything to do with what's actually happening. When it comes down to it, overthinking is code for making shit up.

I can't date a guy who doesn't like me enough to text me back. He must not care about my feelings. I bet he thinks I'm too opinionated or too career motivated or something. Maybe he doesn't feel comfortable that I make more money than he does. I bet he's dating other people. Maybe he's a player. Maybe he doesn't want a relationship at all. But maybe he's my soulmate. Would my soulmate make me wait like this? The universe doesn't work like that, does it? Maybe he's just a Capricorn. Oh God, can I really date a Capricorn?! *OK, I just looked on Facebook, and he's not a Capricorn, but now I need to learn more about Pisces. Have I ever dated another Pisces?!*

I know I'm not the only woman who's done this. How much time have we all wasted on this insanity throughout our lives?

If I'm completely honest, the reason I got stuck overthinking during my first dates with Jay was my extreme lack of confidence when it came to dating and romantic relationships, specifically. I'd had bad breakups, been heartbroken, and dated all the wrong men for all the wrong reasons. My past made me think I couldn't trust myself, and I was terrified of being hurt again. I'm thrilled it all worked out, of course, but also sad to think I wasted so much time and energy on issues that didn't exist when I could have spent those moments invested in my life, as well as being better connected with him. I'm determined not to let that happen now in other areas of my life. There's a better, more confident way to live than in that spiral.

THE ANTIDOTE TO OVERTHINKING IS ACTION

Action builds confidence and eliminates overthinking. If you take nothing else away from this book, please believe me when I say that action is the stuff of confidence-building. You can't think, hope, or fingers-and-toes cross your way into it. You must act your way into confidence through the risks you take, no matter how small, that build up over time and yield big gains in the end. If we want to get out of our heads and make things happen, we have to get into action far sooner than we typically feel ready. Understandably, this can feel terrifying—or, at the very least, uncomfortable. Don't panic, though. I'm not suggesting you jump into the deep end of the pool without knowing how to swim. My suggestion for embarking on any task that feels overwhelming is break it down into smaller action steps.

Imagine, for a moment, that I want to climb Mt. Everest and am standing at the bottom, intimidated as I look up. (I have no aspirations of doing this, by the way. I barely like hiking. I can only assume, though, that it would be daunting.) How does anyone climb Mt. Everest? The only answer is, "One step at a time." But I'm guessing no one just wakes up one day, picks up some equipment, and starts climbing, expecting to reach the summit. That would be overwhelming and, frankly, physically impossible. There are action steps I would need to take to climb the world's tallest mountain. Notice that I said *action* steps, not *thinking* steps. I might begin building my endurance by working out on a regular schedule. I might start by hiking on a local hill, having a conversation with someone who loves to climb, or joining a climbing group. The point is, there are tons of smaller steps I could take to get into action toward accomplishing that big scary goal. And at the end of the day, it would take a lot of practice to do that huge, seemingly crazy, insurmountable thing. None of it would happen at all unless I got up and got going, one frickin' foot in front of the other.

OK, so *how* do we do this? I mean, I can't really go through a chapter on action and not give you action steps, can I? You might remember that I touched on this process briefly in chapter six. For those of you who are how-to junkies like me, here are some tactics that can help break the cycle of overthinking and get you into action faster than if left to your own devices.

Step 1: List all the worst-case scenarios you can think of.

Do it with a limit in mind so you don't get caught in the overthinking trap. This limit could be an amount, like ten things, or a time, like thirty minutes. Then apply the same limit, and write down all the best things that could happen or the best-case scenarios.

Let's pretend I want to climb Mt. Everest (again, I don't) and have limited myself to five things. Worst case: I could die. I might lose a limb. I'd have to sacrifice a lot of my time training, which would mean giving up on other things. I might not make it to the top, and be embarrassed. And I probably would have to stop eating so much cheese. Best case: I could say I did something very few people have ever done. I'd be so proud of myself. I'd be in the best shape of my life.[21] And I'd probably meet some new and really cool people in the process of training.

---

[21] Hello, summit picture! I'd blast that everywhere and show literally every person I came into contact with. Watch me picking up the dry cleaning like, "Have you seen me at the top of Mt. Everest?!?"

Step 2: Ask yourself which list is more compelling, meaningful, and connected to what's important to you.

I'm not gonna lie, my best-case list is making me think climbing Everest could be a good idea; but I also know it's not something I truly desire. However, it is making me realize I should come up with something similar, on a much smaller scale. This kind of realization may happen for you. Maybe in going through this process, the big goal still seems too daunting. If you're even remotely excited about what you wrote down, you can take action steps toward it without totally committing. We call this a test.

Step 3: Assuming the thing you're thinking about is meaningful, or at the very least that you'd like to test it, begin writing down action steps.

Write down anything and everything you can think of, within a limit, like an hour, a day, or a week. If 70 percent or more of the things on that list are doable for you, then go for it. You're ready. Any more time thinking about it will be wasted time. Trust yourself that you'll figure out the other 30 percent as you go! But if you start writing action steps and you realize that less than 40 percent of them seem doable, then start small and simultaneously test and grow your list. In my Everest example, I don't even know where I'd start. I can think of about fifteen things I could do, but I'm guessing there are 1,500 things that I don't even know about. And of the fifteen things

I do know about, only a couple seem doable to me. So I'd start with one, and get into action.

People often ask me, "How can you speak in front of thousands of people? I'd never be able to do that." My answer is simple: "I didn't *start* by speaking in front of thousands of people." And it's true. I started by speaking in front of training groups of three or four people, tops. I was the most prepared and the most nervous and the most excited and the most worried I could possibly be, but I didn't overthink it to the point of inaction. I didn't talk myself out of it due to nervousness. I showed up and did the thing and although it didn't go perfectly, I learned from the experience and did a better job the next time. Over time, the rooms were filled with ten to twenty-five people, and then a hundred, and so on. I can't say public speaking is a total piece of cake, but it's certainly not as nerve-wracking as it used to be. I still get nervous, no matter the size of the room I'm speaking to, because I care. I want to do a great job! But I've also learned that being slightly underprepared compared to where I think I should be is when I deliver at my best.

If we believe that practice makes progress, then action is the strategy we use to build confidence—to trust our inner knowing and our ability. It's the way we *demonstrate* that trust. Think of it like proof. I can say I trust myself until I'm blue in the face, but when I get into action, I'm showing myself that I do. Action is an opportunity for us to practice and grow, regardless of the outcome, and requires us to be in progress toward what really matters.

WE ALL HAVE TWO CHOICES

Success coach Jim Rohn once said, "We must all suffer from one of two pains: the pain of discipline or the pain of regret." My twist on that is we all need to *choose* between two pains: the pain of action, or the pain of regret. Which will you choose?

If you choose to act, you will build confidence and minimize regret. If you choose to overthink and remain in inaction, not only will you live with regrets, you'll also likely not be any closer to living the life you want. In those moments of doubt when you're terrified of not being ready, remind yourself: 100 percent ready is not a thing, ever. Getting over that thought is the key to improving at every skill or talent in existence. Women have every right to raise our hands and put ourselves out there at the same rate as our male counterparts do. That company should be made aware that you want that job. You should run for that election. Go apply for that scholarship. Get after that promotion and let them know why you deserve it. You are here for a reason, and you have so much to contribute. We would all benefit from a little less thinking and a little more doing. Less worrying and more trusting. Less wondering and more joy. The next time you find yourself worrying endlessly, stop thinking so much and get moving! They're called *action* heroes for a reason...and the best news is you can be an *action* hero, too. Bring on the capes!

Seriously, I think we should start an action squad and, at the very least, get jackets. When you think about what would be possible in our lives if we took all the time we spend overthinking and rein-vested it into action, we might actually take over the world. And while world domination isn't a goal of mine, it could be fun. But we would have to let go of overthinking, perfectionism, and head trash... which, for many of us, revolves around comparing ourselves to others. *If I'm not performing better than he is at work, I'll never get ahead in my career.* Comparing ourselves to others and judging ourselves in the process is a common practice we all participate in, which brings us to our next confidence derailer...

ACTIVITY RECAP

An Exercise for Combatting Overthinking

STEP 1: List all the worst-case and best-case scenarios you can think of within a defined limit.

STEP 2: Ask yourself which list is more compelling, meaningful, and connected to what's important to you.

STEP 3: Begin writing down action steps. If 70 percent or more of the things on that list are doable for you, go for it.

REMEMBER: 100 percent ready is never a thing!

CHAPTER 9

Comparison, Judgment, and Choosing Confidence

"Don't compare your behind the scenes to somebody else's highlight reel."

—STEVEN FURTICK

I'D LIKE YOU TO TAKE A MOMENT to picture a woman who's just waking up in the morning. We'll call her Jane, but Jane is you. Jane is any of us, because we've all been in her shoes (or PJs, in this case). She grabs her phone to turn off her alarm, stretches and yawns, but doesn't get up. Instead, she checks her email and starts scrolling through social media. She's curious about what's happening out in the world today—what may have come up at work in the last eight hours, how her friends and family are feeling, or what drama has occurred. Within seconds of scanning the posts on her feed, she feels simultaneously better and worse about herself. Better, because at least she's not a complete moron like that person who commented on that post, or living back at home like her friend from high school. Worse, because she feels she's not rich enough to be traveling to Bali like someone on her feed; fit enough to post a picture of her perfectly toned-yet-not-at-all-sweaty post-workout body like the influencer she follows; or as put together as the co-worker she'll have lunch with later. Jane was well-rested and ready to start her day five minutes ago, but now has a thousand thoughts swirling through her head about herself and all these different people, some of whom she hasn't even actually met or spoken with in decades. Just like that, she starts the day with her confidence derailed.

These days we're inundated with information about other people's lives, what they're doing, what they're accomplishing, and how they look... or at least what versions of those things they want us to see. I know that judging other people and comparing ourselves to them existed twenty years ago, but I doubt there's ever been a time in history when it was as accessible and easy of a trap to fall into. It's now a regular part of our day-to-day lives, just a finger swipe away, to waste our time and energy competing in our own minds with everyone else.

OUR MENTAL JUNK FOOD IS HURTING US

I know I can't keep JJ off social media forever, but by God, I'm going to try for as long as I possibly can. Without exception, every successful person, professional influencer, or business owner I've asked has said they don't want their kid on social media. We feel this way because we know it's ultimately not good for us. We're addicted and, generally speaking, addictions aren't healthy. One of the many reasons we crave social media is because of those fleeting, temporary moments of validation that cause us to feel good about ourselves. "Look how many people liked my status. I must have said or done something important! Look how many views and comments I got. People really like me. God, what is she wearing? So glad I have the sense not to go out in public looking like that. Man, that guy's an idiot. So glad I'm not that stupid..." We validate ourselves through likes, comments, and followers and make ourselves feel better by looking down on others. But *none* of that is confidence. It's insecurity, ego, and arrogance.

We have moments of feeling terrible as we scroll. We don't feel as beautiful as other people, or accomplished, or intelligent, or popular, or cool. All the issues we internally struggle with bubble to the surface and get right in our head as we absorb how other people are living. We think there's something wrong with us, that we could and should be doing better in a million different ways, and our insecurity grows louder and more aggressive. The head trash heaps upon itself, polluting our mind with filth. We feel like shit, and we're not really sure why because most of this is unraveling subconsciously. It's almost impossible to log on and stay neutral. We all know this is happening and can feel it chipping away at our confidence daily.

WHAT WE'RE COMPARING OURSELVES TO DOESN'T EXIST

What happens on social media is not real. It's make-believe. A version of a story. A piece of a bigger picture. It's pretend, like the movies I watch with my daughter on the couch. But that's not how we relate to it, is it? When we get on our platform of choice, we begin to compare our everyday life, our "behind the scenes," with someone else's best moments—their "highlight reel." I often say it's like comparing apples to airplanes because we're not even comparing similar things. We only see the things people are proudest of or most excited about. Even when we're privy to the bad parts, we hear about them from the benefit of hindsight. "This is what happened to me a month ago. Here's how I've recovered from the experience and what I learned from it." And then, somehow, we have the audacity to feel bad about ourselves and make ourselves out to be bad, wrong, too much, or too little, knowing damn well we're comparing our full story with their incomplete information.

We will never get the full picture of someone else's story, yet we still compare and follow up with judgment. We do this offline, too. I remember a woman I met years ago who was older, more established, and further along in her career. In my mind, she had so much capacity, and I couldn't even begin to understand how she was accomplishing everything she was. I couldn't wrap my brain around her energy and all the things she had on her plate. "How does she do that? Why can't I do that too?" I started feeling bad about myself and wondering what was wrong with me. I started taking on more tasks, thinking, "If she can do it, so can I." It wasn't until a couple years later, as our friendship deepened, that I realized *certain* aspects of her life were amazing, but others weren't going well at all. She dealt with massive insecurities of her own that I could never have imagined from the outside looking in. She was dealing with heavy personal challenges I'd known nothing about. Our brains are always trying to fill in the blanks of situations we don't understand, but when we get to know people, it's always the same eventually. "Ah. They're human." Of course they are. Just like you and me.

I've wasted a lot of time and energy playing the comparison-and-judgment game, feeling unworthy—when in fact, I wasn't making a fair comparison in the first place. Instinctually, we know on some level that everyone suffers and has moments of doubt, fear, and failure; but our minds don't focus on that when we're measuring ourselves against them. We think that if something is going well for someone, their life must be all good. If they're making a ton of money, that person must be happy. If they're achieving a certain level of success, they must have it all figured out. If they're attractive in our eyes, they must have the best relationship. None of these correlations is necessarily true, and I know from experience in this field that if someone's trying to prove or tell you how successful or confident they are, you probably shouldn't believe them. Remember, confidence is usually quiet, while arrogance is loud, and insecurity feels the need to prove itself.

Let me say a quick thing about judgment's and comparison's annoying little cousins, complaining and gossiping. They're bad news. Nothing good ever happens when you hang out with them. They make you look bad just by being with them. In all seriousness, these are absolutely confidence derailers. Complaining is talking about something you don't have the courage to *do* anything about.[22] Gossiping is saying things about someone you don't have the confidence to say to their face.

The counterintuitive discovery that's important with all of these derailers is that, whether you're doing it to yourself or someone else, it chips away at *your* confidence. I think that's pretty easy to see when we're our own target. When we're judging ourselves and thinking we come up short, feeling less-than, or thinking we're not enough, we can feel it in our bodies causing us pain. But when we're looking at others and thinking about how horrible they are for whatever it is they're doing, we're still doing damage to our own confidence! Crazy, right? The reason judging someone else chips away at your confidence is because you're feeding your inner critic and your brain doesn't actually care which direction the judgment is going. All it cares about is that it has been fed. It's only a matter of time until that judgment turns back on you. Judgments always give us more insight into the person judging than they do the person being judged. Your judgments say more about you than anyone else. Yikes!

---

[22] Credit to Lisa Kalmin for that gem.

COMPARISON, JUDGMENT, AND CHOOSING CONFIDENCE

It's true, *our* judgment is a representation of *our* values, perceptions, maturity, beliefs, and interpretations. We're projecting all the time. No matter how self-righteous we feel when we're pointing fingers, we're ultimately doing damage to our confidence as a whole.

THE ANTIDOTE TO COMPARISON
AND JUDGMENT IS CHOOSING CONFIDENCE

"...What?"

Yes, you read that right. You have to choose it.

"If it were that easy, Nicole, I wouldn't be reading this book, would I?!"

Let me explain and make this very important distinction. A lot of us think confidence is a feeling we either have or don't have. We feel like it comes to us or it doesn't. It somehow arrives or it fails us. Like, I woke up this morning feeling confident, or I didn't. I'm going to walk into this opportunity if I feel confident... and if I don't, I'm gonna wait. It's like confidence chooses *us* (or doesn't), not the other way around. It's kind of like a bad relationship... We're waiting for confidence to decide it wants to be with us, all the while forgetting that we get to choose whether we want to be with it. It's all wrong, I tell you!

It's incredibly important to understand that confidence isn't just a feeling. It's a choice. Most of us have it backward. We *generate* confidence. It's created within us. It's not just a feeling that shows up and suddenly provides the empowerment we've been missing. We have to *choose* and then demonstrate it by taking action. It really is that simple. But like so many things that are simple, that doesn't mean it's easy. It takes practice. (Are you sensing a theme yet?)

One of my favorite experiences related to the work I do around confidence is the many, many opportunities I get to witness women choose it, even in those moments when they aren't feeling it. I've seen women do speaking engagements in front of hundreds of people after just coming out of a horrible week. I've watched women pull themselves together and call an A+ prospective client they've been avoiding reaching out to for months. I've known women who walked into sales meetings and landed their biggest clients after having just been rejected. I've witnessed and experienced women being heartbroken and then deciding to put themselves out there again. The list is endless here... You probably have examples in your life where you've made these choices. You're probably doing it far more often than you give yourself credit for!

Entrepreneurs do this on a regular basis. When starting out, or launching a new product or service, the results they hope for aren't happening yet. They're nervous, wrestling with doubt, and having moments where they feel like it's all going to fall apart; but somehow they keep boldly moving forward regardless. I'm so inspired when I see it because I know they're creating pride and trust in themselves.

We've all heard or been told to "Fake it 'til you make it." I'm not a big fan of faking anything and hate this advice.[23] This may seem like semantics, but I think the difference is of the utmost importance. I'd encourage you instead to "Choose it until you feel it." Choose confidence over and over again, minute by minute if you need to, and keep choosing it until the feeling catches up. As you do this, you'll begin to gather more evidence of your awesomeness with each instance of choosing confidence, and you'll build that pride and trust in yourself, which will make it easier to be confident.

I'm not a big sports person, but I notice people choosing confidence any time I watch any game, whether it be team or individual. Jay's a big basketball fan, and while I don't know a ton about the sport, what I do notice is that the players are in the moment, making and missing shots. They have plays that don't go as planned all the time. They constantly have other players in their face, fiercely defending while the crowd cheers and jeers. Do they go stand in a corner and let other people's judgments consume them? Do they say, "I'm not playing as good as the other person in my position, so I'm just gonna sit this one out"? Do they worry that they're a failure and let fear and doubt take over? No. They *can't*. They choose confidence, play by play, over and over again. They take the next shot like the last one never happened. They immediately run back to defend whether they get the points or not. I'm always in awe of how they practice choosing confidence, every time. They don't get

---

[23] We women have been faking far too much for far too long!

to give up when they lose a game. They choose confidence for the next practice and the next game after that. This is just one example from the athletic sphere, but people around us are choosing confidence all the time, and we can take a page from their playbook. Again, you're probably doing this in your own life more than you notice or give yourself credit for.

You may have chosen confidence at work without even noticing it. Most of our jobs demand that we do. Maybe you started the day off on a bad note, like running late and missing the school bus and cursing in front of your and your neighbor's child. (Or maybe that just happened to me.) Or maybe you just had a conversation with a colleague who isn't pulling their weight on a project that didn't go the way you hoped it would. You have another meeting on your calendar in ten minutes, however, and there's no time to marinate in how bad you feel about it, or them. You have to brush it off and choose confidence to keep moving forward. You have to stay rooted in your purpose and focus on what's next. Onward and upward. Taking your feelings, judgments, comparisons, and head trash into the next meeting will throw you off your game, and that's simply not an option. This strength and ability to choose something even if we're not feeling it can be carried with us into all areas of our lives.

So how do we practice this? How do we choose confidence over judgment or comparison? How do we build on it? Friends, there are so many ways to do it. I'm going to give you a few that have worked for me and others, but know that this is not an exhaustive list.

Tip 1: Create, find, or use a mantra.

Whether you prefer to call it a mantra, an affirmation, a catchphrase, or a declaration, what's important is that you have one! It should be a few words, or one to two sentences max. You want to keep it short enough that you can both remember and use it quickly when needed. Here are a few mantra-building tips: use I or My (not we), say it in the present tense (because you're calling the future into the present), have it be meaningful to you, and eliminate any wishy-washy words. Don't worry about grammar, whether it will sound good to others, or if it feels cheesy or too big. This is for you, and you only.

Here are some mantra (or whatever you want to call it) examples:

When you see someone else crushing it and start feeling bad about yourself.

You can say *I am enough, just as I am.*

Someone gives you unsolicited business advice?

My goals are mine, and they matter. I confidently achieve them.

If someone questions your abilities?

I am an unstoppable force.

When someone judges you or comments negatively about your choices?

I trust myself.

Tip 2: Use Mel Robbins' Five-Second Rule.

When you catch yourself hesitating on something you want to do that requires confidence, count 5-4-3-2-1 and move forward on 1.

This is especially helpful for interrupting the habit of overthinking, and interrupting fear and doubt. Basically, it's a quick method to change your mental habits and get out of your comfort zone! For example, if you have an idea in a meeting but don't normally speak up, 5-4-3-2-, and on 1, say your idea (or raise your hand if blurting your idea out would be bad timing).

Tip 3: Practice intentional breathing.

Take three deep breaths with purpose… Center and ground yourself, breathe in what you need, and breathe out everything else. For example: plant your feet firmly on the floor, put your hands on your hips or in prayer position, close your eyes, breathe in confidence, and breathe out doubt. Then open your eyes and get into action.

Tip 4: Build and leverage a Recovery Plan.

This is something I developed as a way for me to get back into action on the tough days, especially when I find myself stuck in comparison or judgment of myself or others. Because, let's be honest, it's pretty easy to take action on the great days! But when the shit hits the fan, you've just faced rejection, fear and doubt have taken control of your brain, or when you just don't feel like it, it's important to have a plan. Your Recovery Plan is a list of things that give you energy, remind you of what's important, motivate you, and are action-oriented. Taking one or more actions that fuel you will get you in the right place to take action when you don't feel like it or are afraid to. You can find a free guide to Designing Your Recovery Plan on my website, www.nicolekalil.com, but here are some examples of things that you'll find there:

- *Read your Feel-Good Folder:* This is where you keep any notes that people send you telling you about the great work you've done, or how you've made a difference, and so on. It will help you focus on yourself again rather than anyone else.
- *Listen to your Confidence Playlist:* Create and name a playlist that includes songs that fire you up! It's nineties gangsta rap for me. (Seriously.)
- *Exercise:* Go for a run, get on the treadmill, do yoga, go on a hike, or take a boxing class. Do anything that releases endorphins, connects you to your strength, and can help you release negative energy or frustration. Sometimes, you just need to hit something.
- *Read:* This could be something faith-based, like The Bible, or self-development oriented. It could be quotes, blogs, or books…doesn't matter as long as it fuels you in the best way.
- *Listen:* Podcasts are a great option here! I know a good one (shameless plug for my podcast, *This Is Woman's Work*— you can find it on Apple, Spotify, or wherever you listen to podcasts! OK, shameless plug over.).

- *Phone a Friend:* Know what you need, and call the best person to give it to you. Do *not* call someone who's going to let you wallow in your misery or commiserate in your judgments. Call someone like a coach, a mentor, or a friend who's an encourager, cheerleader, or challenger.

There are so many more options here, but you get the idea! Do as many things on your Recovery Plan as needed to get you back into action toward what matters.

CHOOSING CONFIDENCE ON PURPOSE

Why is choosing confidence the antidote to judgment and comparison? Because it's a fast, simple way to shift your mindset away from everyone else and back to what matters. We need that when we find ourselves playing the comparison game and when we're judging ourselves and others. How can you practice it while you're scrolling online, seeing pictures of your friends on vacation in Bora Bora? I might argue (and I'm testing this out myself with occasional social-media detoxes) that choosing confidence might involve not getting on social media in the first place. I wouldn't go as far as to claim confident people don't use social media, because they certainly do. Ask yourself, though, what are you looking to accomplish by getting that fix? What's your purpose, and are you honoring it by logging on? How will seeing what other people are up to serve you?

Are you currently in the right place for it? Only you can provide the true answers to those questions, but I submit that it's beneficial to set an intention rather than just scarfing down that mental junk food. If you're mindful about what's entering your headspace, you'll be far less likely to be derailed and feel your confidence take a hit. But when you do jump on social media, practice choosing confidence like an athlete—moment by moment, play by play. Choose confidence.

One of the funniest (and most frustrating) things about social media to me is how often people spread disinformation about what confidence is. You and I know by now it's not about comments, likes, or views. It's not about how it looks; it's about how it is. Confidence is built from the inside out, and we'll talk in the next chapter about how to keep ours solid.

ACTIVITY RECAP

Methods for Choosing Confidence

TIP 1: Create, find, or use a mantra.

TIP 2: Use Mel Robbins' Five-Second Rule.

TIP 3: Practice intentional breathing.

TIP 4: Build and leverage a Recovery Plan.

Which of these tips will work best for you?

CHAPTER 10

Seeking Confidence Externally and Building It Internally

*"If outside validation is your only source
of nourishment, you will hunger
for the rest of your life."*

—UNKNOWN

IMAGINE THAT SOMEONE out in the world is walking around with your confidence, but you don't know who it is. They've got it in their pocket or hidden in their bag, and life's not-so-fun game is that you need to find them and get them to give it to you. Maybe it's the person you've got a crush on or one of your best friends. Maybe it's the bully who made fun of you, or a complete stranger you meet at a bar after work. Maybe it's your boss, who has it hidden in their desk drawer and is waiting to present it to you alongside your pro-motion. Could it be someone at the gym? Maybe it's your parents, and they've been secretly withholding it from you this whole time. (Shout-out to parents playing the long game!) Maybe your confi-dence is hiding in a wedding ring box, the glove compartment of a luxury car, or your child's dirty little palm. All you have to do to win the confidence con is figure out who or what has it, like some incessant game of *Where's Waldo?* But once you find it, you still have to prove yourself worthy—the right clothes, the right car, the right job, the right house, the right marriage, or the right number on the scale—and they'll hand it over so you can finally feel good about yourself.

Does this sound like a game you'd want to play? Of course not. It's ridiculous, but so many of us *are* playing this game and operat-ing as if it's how confidence works. Remember the false equation I introduced at the beginning of the book? "If X happens, then I'll feel confident." We think someone or something else will give it to us, but it never has worked this way, and it never will. Trusting yourself is not a "If you go first, I'll do it, too," proposition. There isn't anyone or anything to prove yourself to, wait for, or find.

True confidence is built internally and involves one person. We've been conned into seeking it from all the wrong sources, especially as women. In this chapter, we're going to cover this topic in a bit more depth and talk about specific strategies for building real confidence from the inside. The empowering kind that's based on trust, isn't conditional, and can't be taken away. The kind that's solely in our hands, not hiding from us.

WE'VE BEEN FED A LOT OF BULLSHIT

Advertising, television, movies, and the media—especially social media, today—play a huge part in the spread of false information about confidence; but they only shoulder some of the blame. The patriarchy, religion, gender expectations, cultures, work environments, well-intentioned family and friends (and not-so-well-intentioned family and friends), lovers, strangers, influencers, authors, and so on, have misrepresented confidence so frequently that one can't help but be confused. In a lot of cases, they lied to you about confidence because they were lied to, as well. But at the end of the day, your confidence is yours, and you get to decide what is true for you.

One of the many reasons I hate social media is because I can't scroll without coming across an ad, an influencer, or a friend conveying the idea that something will bring women confidence that won't. Another reason is I can't stand Instagram reels. (I'm sorry if you do them and love them, but mostly I just want to cover my eyes before they start to bleed. Anyway, that's a me thing.) I've seen confidence building tips like,

"Work out! Lose weight!"

"Take this course and make millions!"

"Smile more!"

"Go get your hair done!"

"Achieve this goal!"

"Find the person of your dreams!"

"Get engaged and show pictures of your ring!"

"Boost your image!"

"Dress for success!"

What most of these things have in common is a particular focus on the need for external validation. This isn't just a social media thing, but an advertising thing as well. Whole teams tirelessly work behind the scenes at companies to study the psychology of consumers and figure out how to lure us in. If you buy this car, use this product, drink this drink, carry this phone, shop at this store, wear this label, have this body type, it will bring you confidence. It's in the clothes you wear, the makeup you buy,[24] or the gym you join. If you do or get those things, you'll get the validation you seek, and then somehow you'll be able to trust yourself more?

But they get us with this crap, don't they? Because on the other side of the "confidence" they're asking us to buy is the life of our dreams. The person of our dreams. The perfectly behaved kids. Our perfect body. The promotion. The higher income. The compliments. The adoration. The feeling that we matter.

---

[24] "Maybe she's born with it?" If it's confidence you're talking about, then yes. If it's long eyelashes, it probably is indeed Maybelline.

Ninety-two percent of people who get cosmetic surgery are female, but is that about trust or is that about societal expectations of how women should look and age? I ask that without judgment as someone who dyes my hair and spends a crap-ton of money on face lotions. I'm not saying you shouldn't get Botox or buy the mascara or get the cosmetic surgery. By all means, do as you wish! But if you're doing it because you think it'll make you feel confident, it won't.

A lot of the time, we also absorb the message that if we feel good, attractive, or validated, we're going to feel confident. And let me say again, there is nothing wrong with wanting to feel good or attractive! Validation *does* feel good. But all those things are the icing on the confidence cake, not the cake itself. For example, if I got dressed up for dinner and my husband said I looked smoking hot, would that make me feel good? Sure it would! Would it make me feel *confident,* though? Absolutely not. I love my husband, but Jay's not walking around with my confidence in his pocket, and I'm not waiting for him to give it to me. Feeling attractive is great but does nothing to help me trust myself more. Confidence has no correlation to our culture's obsession with happiness, feeling good all the time, how we look, what people think of us, or how stubbornly we're supposed to try to convince others we're awesome. What often ends up happening is we feel like we *need* validation. And now validation owns us, and we don't know who we are without it—which, of course, was never confidence at all.

You might be thinking, "But Nicole, dressing a certain way for a professional event actually makes me feel confident!" I'd argue what you really feel is ready, prepared, energized, or even superstitious (hello, lucky shirt!). I have a routine I go through whenever I speak and am very conscious of what I wear. I want to send the right message, engage people, and walk on that stage feeling like a million bucks. But that's not the same as trusting myself. I guarantee you I could walk on a stage and deliver a phenomenal presentation in my sweats…possibly an even better one than usual, because I'd be super comfy. I can be confident and look like a million bucks, but one is not a requirement of the other.

I do want to address one category that falls into a gray area for me. We're told consistently that if we do this it will give us confidence, and in some cases it's absolutely true, but in others it's absolutely not. This gray area is working out. *So* many people say that working out makes them feel confident. Every exercise guru or program tells you it will, and every gym considers or uses confidence as a selling point. Does working out actually build confidence? Yes and no. It depends on why and how you're doing it. If you're doing it to lose weight to fit in a certain size or be toned in your bikini so you attract attention and look great in the eyes of others, it's probably not going to help you trust yourself. Said another way, if your primary goal is external (e.g., I'm going to post a picture of my rockin' body on Instagram), it's probably not confidence you'll get. You might feel good, you might feel attractive, and I say good for you! But you also might feel like your body is never good enough and that you always have more pounds or inches to lose—or, even worse, you could develop body dysmorphia or an eating disorder. *But,* if your goal is health and well-being, if you're working out to *feel* good, increase energy, and take care of yourself, then it can absolutely build confidence. Why? Because you're developing trust in yourself. Trust that you'll take care of, prioritize, and value yourself. Trust in your strength, your commitment, and your growth. Trust that you can do hard and uncomfortable things and make it out alive and feeling proud. Working out builds confidence when you keep your word to yourself, get into action, and show up to do the work. We've all had that experience where you feel like a goddess after one workout. Did that one workout actually change anything about you externally? Nope. What it did was change something internally... It created pride, power, and strength. Those things are absolutely confidence builders.

The true equation, the one that actually works, is "When I'm confident, I'll have a higher probability of X." When you're confident, and when you trust yourself, you'll be more likely to go after and achieve whatever goal you desire. When you're confident, you'll take the risks, make the decisions, have the conversations, and chase the dreams. Confidence precedes those things, not the other way around. This goes directly against everything we've been told, and it's important to see the lie for what it is.

You're the only person who can choose confidence for yourself. You are the creator, the decider, and the giver of your own confidence.

Sometimes people ask me, "Is that person confident?" My answer: "Only one person knows that for sure, and it's not me." No one else can look and tell what's actually happening inside you. Confidence is not built by collecting external evidence of our worth or value. Validation is for parking. It is not required for confidence. It's time to stop believing in the false equation we all bought into without even knowing it. It's time to stop bending over backward in order to *prove* something. No one you're trying to prove your worth to is carrying your confidence around in their pocket waiting to give it to you—which, if you think about it, is pretty awesome news.

THE ANTIDOTE TO SEEKING CONFIDENCE EXTERNALLY IS BUILDING IT INTERNALLY

There are a lot of ways to go about building true confidence internally, but thinking about how one builds trust is most helpful. How do you build trust in your relationships with others? How do others build trust with you? Think about it, because here we're turning it around on ourselves. The processes work in much the same way.

Do you trust yourself? It may have been a long time since you thought about that, but I'd argue it's one of the most important questions you can ask. Because if you don't trust yourself, who will? There's only ever going to be one person who gets to live your life, and that's you. Given that fact, wouldn't it make sense to love and trust yourself? And if you love and trust yourself, wouldn't you increase the probability of attracting people into your life that also love, trust, respect, and value you? While we don't need other people to validate us, as human beings we are wired for connection. We want and need to share our lives, experiences, and gifts with others. Life becomes a lot better, and a lot easier, if you attract into it good people you can trust. But the best way to do that is to model it for yourself first! We attract who we *are* more than we attract what we *want*.

The good news is that there are many, many ways to build internal trust! I'm going to list several of my favorites, but this list is not meant to be exhaustive. These are just methods I know of that work, and any of us can do them any time we want. So, as we're all looking to build internal trust, and therefore unshakable confidence, here are some great places to start or grow from:

Tip 1: Keep your commitments.

When you ask anyone how someone could earn their trust, they'll answer with some version of, "They'd have to keep their commitments." They do what they say they will, their word matters, and you can count on them. So a phenomenal way to build internal trust is to keep the commitments we make to others *and* the ones we make to ourselves. As women, we tend to be better about honoring the commitments we make to others; we put our internal agreements on the backburner. If it has to do with our family, kids, friends, and our work, we often do what we say we will. But if it's something that impacts only us, we can get pretty loosy-goosy with our word. When you don't follow through on the commitments you make to yourself, you're breaking trust and chipping away at your confidence. Important note here: as a society, we've become hyper-obsessed with making commitments. Not everything needs to be a commitment. There are goals, habits, or things we're trying out and testing. Our commitments are the *promises* we make to ourselves and others, and authentic trust is built when we keep them. So be careful what you commit to, and that you don't overcommit. It's OK to say, "This is a goal," or "I'll do my best," or "I'm going to test this out and see if it works for me." But if you choose to give your word? Well, then, keeping it is going to mean the difference between building trust or losing it. These are the important things that deeply matter and give us the belief that we can count on ourselves. Another point here... This is not about perfection. You are human, and you'll let yourself and others down on occasion. Your opportunity here is to give yourself grace, practice forgiveness, learn, grow, and be better next time.

Tip 2: Create and communicate boundaries.

Another way to build internal confidence is to set and communicate healthy boundaries. I've seen over and over that when people communicate their boundaries, it actually increases both trust and respect. But, I hear from so many women that they have a hard time saying no and worry that it'll negatively impact their relationships.

Many of us have been socialized to be people pleasers and martyrs, so we feel like we're never supposed to say no. Every time we say yes to something, however, we're saying no to something else, and it's usually something that matters to us. As an example, you might be asked to head the PTA at your child's school, but you know you'd have no time to read the books or do the workouts you've been wanting to if you did. You might be asked, yet again, to take on another project at work, but you know if you do, you'll have to trade in hours you'd spend with your friends or family. In those moments, we have a hard time saying no, often because we feel selfish or feel like we're disappointing someone. But the reality is you'll either disappoint them or yourself. An even bigger reality is that in saying no, you may gain your own respect and theirs. Again, your relationship with you is the most important one you'll ever take part in. When you say yes to opportunities and offers you don't actually want, your trust for yourself will crumble. If saying "yes" automatically is a problem for you, you might practice how to say "no" or "maybe" in ways that feel comfortable. Plan out what you'll say ahead of time, so the next time someone asks, you'll have a prepared response and won't automatically default to, "Sure, I'll do it!" An example could be, "I'm so honored that you thought of me. I need to take some time to see if I can commit to this fully. Follow up with me in a week." Or, "Thank you for thinking of me! Unfortunately, I'm at capacity at the moment, but I'd love to introduce you to someone in my network that would be a great fit for what you're looking for." Having those go-to responses lined up can help us trust ourselves across a spectrum of different situations.

Tip 3: Practice self-care.

Yes, I'm jumping on the self-care bandwagon! However, how self-care is being modeled and encouraged has become a bit of a pet peeve of mine. I'm not talking about getting your hair and nails done or having frequent spa days. If that's self-care to you, great. It's not the entirety of what self-care means, though, and it has an element of privilege that makes it seem like only people with excess time and money can practice self-care. That's not what I mean. I'm talking about things that actually *fill your cup* and bring you energy, and they don't have to be expensive or complicated. Self-care for you might be deep breathing. It might be moving your body, getting outside, or reading a book. For me, it's exercising regularly (even though I hate exercising), reading, and traveling. It's making sure Jay and I have date nights planned and that I get to meet girlfriends a few times a year. (Most of my best friends live across the country, so we need to plan trips.) It's making sure I have time in a week just for myself, which is necessary for me as an introvert. What is it for you? What fills your cup and gives you energy? I'd also like to point out the word "practice" is crucial here, because self-care is ongoing, and practice is how we get better at just about anything. Prioritizing and taking care of yourself is a trust-building activity. Think about it in your relationships. Don't you trust the people who prioritize and take care of you? And you build trust for yourself every time you do it, because you're honoring a commitment you made to yourself—hitting two confidence-building tips in one.

Tip 4: The 3 Ps.

I call my fourth suggestion for building confidence internally the three Ps: Prepare, Plan, and Practice. I pass them on with a word of caution, though, because they will turn into derailers when taken too far. Being prepared is great, but *over*preparing will chip away at your confidence. Having a plan helps, but *over*planning, or being overly attached to the plan, will become problematic. And for the love of all things holy, practice, but keep in mind that the point of practicing is to *do* the thing—so make sure you don't get stuck perpetually practicing. In all three cases, these Ps should lead to action. The 3 Ps are about education, knowledge, and personal and professional development. They create internal trust that you can then execute on. Nervous to meet with your employer to ask for that promotion and raise? Prepare your talking points, plan for possible questions or objections, and practice what you're going to say. Just remember, in order for it to be confidence building, you actually need to go ask for that promotion and raise! Another example that many moms can relate to is having a birthing plan. Pushing a possible seven-plus-pound tiny human out of an even tinier hole is a scary thing for many women. So we take classes or read books to prepare, we create a plan that will help us navigate the situation the best we can, and we even practice breathing or do trial runs to get to the hospital in ten minutes or less. The 3 Ps help you feel ready, but inevitably you'll have to get into action at some point. I've heard so many stories where labor and delivery didn't go according to plan, and in that moment you have to choose trust. Trust yourself, your support team, the doctors...whatever feels right to you. I've learned that the 3 Ps can be incredible confidence builders, but I'd encourage flexibility and action over everything. Rigidity and waiting to be "100 percent ready" is where the 3 Ps end up being counterproductive. How can you make the three Ps work for you?

Tip 5: Be grateful.

Gratitude shifts our mindset away from fear, doubt, and worry toward positive, uplifting emotions. It's shown to improve health, help us overcome adversity, strengthen relationships, and reduce stress. When you practice gratitude, you're choosing to focus your thoughts and build a healthy mindset. When we focus on what we're grateful for, it reinforces the good in our lives, which reminds us we *can* trust ourselves and are capable of creating some pretty awesome things. For all those reasons and more, practicing gratitude will build your confidence!

Tip 6: Speak your truth.

This one may seem obvious, but we trust people who are honest more than we trust people who lie. (Duh.) But honestly, how often in your life are you saying what you mean? Are you honest with the people you live and work with, or do you tell a lot of "harmless white lies?" This is not me giving you permission to say whatever thought flies into your head, but I am encouraging you to be honest with yourself and others. Lies erode trust, and it's pretty important that you speak your truth.

Tip 7: Stand up for yourself.

We covered this briefly in chapter three, but it's worth repeating: Don't let anyone make you feel less-than. Either speak up for yourself or walk away. What you say is far less important than making the choice to let someone know that how they've acted is not OK. I've replayed so many moments, saying "I wish I would've said this or done that," but what makes me feel the absolute worst is when I don't say or do anything at all. Think about if someone was talking badly about you to your best friend or to your mom, and your loved ones didn't say anything at all in your defense or didn't walk away and refuse to participate. You would lose trust. The same goes for when you don't stand up for yourself or walk away when someone says or does something inappropriate, hurtful, or mean.

Tip 8: Be your own hype person.

Encourage, cheer for, celebrate, and motivate yourself the way you would your best friend. Remind yourself of the things you know to be true about *you* at this point in your life. When someone compliments you, say thank you. Don't explain, excuse, or minimize. Better yet, compliment your damn self.

Tip 9: Sleep.

Sleep is so important to our mental, physical, and emotional health. When we don't get enough sleep, we're basically operating throughout our day like a drunk person, and nobody trusts a drunk person. They're not known for their effective decision-making, sound judgment, or wise actions. So ladies, get your sleep! Prioritize it like it's your job... because it is.

Tip 10: Choose your people wisely.

You are the CEO. The boss of your own life. Hire, fire, and promote accordingly, because who you surround yourself with matters. Who you allow into your space will impact your trust in yourself. In business, there's a rule of thumb to hire slowly and fire quickly. Every time I've "fired" someone in my life, my only regret has been wishing I would've done it sooner. Your people are a clear reflection of how you see yourself. It's not only OK to create a better circle, it's encouraged.

THE BENEFITS OF BUILDING TRUE CONFIDENCE ARE ENDLESS

When you make a serious effort to do the work of building real confidence, the benefits you'll experience will impact every area of your life—your career, your family, your relationships, and even your hobbies. You'll enjoy more peace and freedom in your life instead of beating yourself up while seeking external validation. You'll make better decisions. You'll take risks. You'll chase bigger dreams. Building confidence internally is the key we've been searching for all along. The answer was always inside you. It's what makes you feel comfortable in your own skin. It'll help you move forward, seek out what's good for you according to your inner knowing, and walk away from anything or anyone that doesn't serve you. When your confidence is in *your* pocket, you'll know when and how to leave the things that chip away at it behind.

ACTIVITY RECAP

- -

Methods for Building Confidence Internally

TIP 1: Keep your commitments.

TIP 2: Create and communicate boundaries.

TIP 3: Practice self-care.

TIP 4: The 3 Ps.

TIP 5: Be grateful.

TIP 6: Be honest.

TIP 7: Stand up for yourself.

TIP 8: Be your own hype person.

TIP 9: Sleep.

TIP 10: Choose your people wisely.

Take your time and try them all!

Final Thoughts

"Confidence is fidelity to the self."

—Michael Mahoney

You probably started reading this book thinking you knew what confidence was, what it felt like, and what it looked like. I hope you've been able to reconnect with the true definition of the word, which is knowing who you are, owning what you're not, and choosing to embrace all of it. In its simplest form, confidence is the trust we have in and for ourselves. Women have been lied to so much about confidence. It's time to take it back into our own hands, because trust me, it's not living out there anyway. While building our confidence may not solve all the problems of the world, like gender inequality, it's an area where we can make our own individual impact. It's our own little piece of a very large and complex puzzle that we have ownership over. No one can take it away from us unless we let them—and nobody can give it to us, either.

I always think about what could happen in our world if it were filled with more confident women. I firmly believe it would look very different from the way it does today, for the better. That's why I wrote this book. That's why I speak to women and men about confidence. Often, people ask me how to raise confident kids, and my response is always to be a confident parent. Not to be perfect. Not to have it all figured out. Not even to read every parenting book you can get your hands on. Be a parent who chooses confidence, even if you're not feeling it, and who practices trust even when you make mistakes. Demonstrate confidence in a way that ripples out and makes waves the next generation can ride. The answer is the same if you're asking how to create confident employees or teams. Be a confident leader. What would corporate culture look like if women had more confidence? How many women would be raising their hands for the promotions to the C-suite positions? Better yet, how many women would leave corporate cultures or refuse to do business with companies who don't value women in leadership or value pay equity, making those companies lose profit and their competitive edge? How many women would start their own companies and build their own businesses? What would happen with food scarcity, access to healthcare, or issues related to racial inequality in a world of more confident women? My experience is that when women rise, everyone else rises with us.

I know you just want to be happy. We all do. But I also believe that, as a society, we have become overly obsessed with that feeling. This journey isn't about feeling happy all the time, and there's nothing wrong with you if you don't. It isn't about avoiding challenges or pain, because you can't. The important thing is that it's always in our power to *stand* for our happiness; and our confidence is the force that enables us to keep getting back up no matter how many times we fall.

Author Anne Morrow Lindbergh once wrote, "Don't wish me happiness. I don't expect to be happy all the time... Wish me courage and strength and a sense of humor. I will need them all." If that were my quote, I'd add confidence to the list. I wish you confidence, because I know you will need it. We all do.

So, I'll leave you with this: get into action. Whether it's taking the first steps toward a seemingly impossible goal, or taking on the confidence derailer that affects you the most, get proactive and get in motion. Try an exercise or build a habit from this book and see what happens. Remember, this work is always about progress, so don't be discouraged if your whole life isn't transformed overnight. In fact, don't expect that to happen at all. This will always be a journey, and over time you will feel trust building within yourself. There's no use in waiting, because no one is coming to hand your confidence to you, and you can't think your way into it. The time to act is now. Who would you be with more confidence? What risks would you take? What decisions would you make? What dreams would you chase? I say it's time to find out the answers to those questions.

Take this as a loving reminder that you're not alone. I'm right here, climbing that mountain alongside you, and I'll always be cheering you on. There are many, many other women climbing mountains out here with us, putting one foot in front of the other, just like us. When we pass each other, let's give a high-five instead of tearing each other down. Let's leave that comparison and judgment behind. It's too heavy to carry, anyway. We're in this together, and the time has come to see what is possible. We get to create and experiment. We get to *play*, like the confident children we were before the world conned us. Play is silly. It's fun. It's taking risks, big and small, without worrying what everyone will think of our creation. Do *you* like it? If you do, that's all that really matters. If not, the world won't end because of it. You get to try again, as many times as you want, until you feel like you've got it right. You'll be OK, even during the hard parts. Keep choosing confidence. Keep choosing trust.

You've got this. Consider yourself validated.

Acknowledgments

When acknowledging everyone who directly and indirectly helped you do one of the hardest (and best) things you've ever done, do you start with the most important, supportive person? Or do you end with them? First and foremost? Or save the best for last? I'm told I shouldn't rate people on a scale of one to ten or use the star rating system. (I'm not sure why... It works for Yelp). So, I'm going with something like an inverted bell curve, and it's going to be long. Because I'm the author and I get to make my own rules.

I know that confidence doesn't arrive when you marry the man of your dreams (despite what we've been told). I also know that I've never felt more loved, more comfortable in my own skin, and more myself than I do when I'm with you, Jay. I've learned so much about confidence from you. Thank you for choosing to do life with me, for your never-ending support, and for being a man who appreciates my ambition, celebrates my successes, and is slightly amused by my rants. And for reminding me that it's not all that serious. I love you.

JJ, you didn't get a perfect mom. Many days, I'm just doing my best not to mess up too badly. You did get a mom who loves you *all* the time, who picked for you the best dad, and who wants nothing more than for you to live authentically and with opportunity. I hope it's enough. I hope you trust yourself, even if it means rocking the boat with everyone else (including me). I hope my obsession with confidence helps you to hold on to yours whenever life's challenges try to shake it.

Quite literally nothing would be possible without my mom and dad. Mom, I'm forever grateful I got to come to this world through you. Dad, I've never doubted, for one second, that you love me. I wish more girls had that from their dads.

Danielle & Waid—my real sister who I tried to convince was adopted, and my adopted brother who is as real as it gets. Thank you for letting me practice everything on you first and for loving me no matter how many times I got it wrong. Without you, who else would I make fun of mom and dad with? #tootle #JustPeeOnIt.

Pat & Carolyn, nothing confirms your superior intelligence and impeccable decision- making more than your choice of spouses. I love having you in my family, and I feel safer knowing you're taking care of my people.

The entire Kalil clan, if I could've done a worldwide search to handpick my in-laws and the people they married, I couldn't have found any better. I hit the family jackpot.

My father-in-law, Anthony, thank you for raising men who respect, value, and adore confident women. And for keeping us all well fed. Nancy, for loving us all the same.

Tante Lene, for being the first person to show me what it is to respect mother earth, question politicians, live simply, and nourish yourself in every way. Your notes have always been filled with everything I needed to hear.

As an introvert, making new friends is hard for me. I basically depend on kind extroverts to adopt me and not give up when I say no to doing things. It also explains why I've known many of my friends most of my life.

Nikki, my blanket fort friend. I'm grateful I don't remember a time where you weren't in my life. You make *This Is Woman's Work* a real podcast (without you, it'd just be me ranting into a mic) and have always supported my purpose. Being on the receiving end of *your* purpose is one of my life's greatest gifts.

Kim, for being the one that gets me. Never needing to explain, knowing you'll see the best in me, even when I'm showing up at my worst, and for letting me be part of your family. O, thanks for laughing with (at?) me, and always looking out for me, too. Mina, I've loved you from the second you were born. Max, you, too.

Tiffany, there are plenty of times you should have given up on me, but you never do. Thank you for loving so big that you say what needs to be said, and for sticking around to help pick up any pieces. And for laughing with me at all the bullshit life brings.

Julie, for being someone who makes me laugh til I pee. Kate, Chantel, Lesle, Jess, Courtney, for helping me experience the magic that happens when women come together and support each other.

Lynn, first for being there for Jay, and also for me. You are the most thoughtful and caring badass I know. My East Coast friends, for making me feel at home. To Heather Monahan for being real, honest, and a true friend in such a short time. I will always be a huge fan of yours! And Gina DeVee for your support and incredibly generous spirit.

Thanks to everyone on the publishing team who helped me figure out how to write a book... You made a life goal into a real thing! Peggy Holsclaw, for your time, your talent, and for helping me sift through the ideas and somehow seeing a book in them... I wouldn't have this without you.

Special thanks to Bianca Pahl, my ever-patient publishing manager, and my editor, Barbara Boyd, for making sure it all makes sense. The greatest cover designers, Natalie Sowa and Cristina Ricci. And to Skyler Gray, who helped me turn random words and thoughts into a title that I love.

To the women of NM whom I've had the honor to work with... There are far too many of you to name, but every one of you played a part in me living my purpose. Your courage to succeed in a male-dominated industry, your commitment to your clients leading financially secure lives, and your dedication to your own growth is inspiring. I will never stop cheering for you! And a quick shout-out to the women AND men of 029 and 109... Thank you for letting me be part of it. To the Woburn crew... Make it so they all #FeelTheBurn.

Thank you to Ben Newman and the team at BNC Speakers, Julie

O'Keefe at APB Speakers Bureau, and the SHRM Speakers Bureau for helping me to get the message of confidence out to the world!

Kurt Kersey, and the team at Thirty21, for making me look good (and even more amazing, for making it look like I know what I'm doing), and for supporting businesses that the world needs. But mostly for your friendship. You are a good egg.

I'm inspired by many people, but Brené Brown, Glennon Doyle, Adam Grant, and Michelle Obama make it to the top of that list. I'm hoping we'll get to collaborate somehow at some point in my life. If you're reading this and have a connection to them, introducing me will earn you VIP status in my blanket fort for life.

Alex, for helping to keep me sane.

Mark G, The Wine Guy in Zionsville, IN, for also keeping me sane, but in a totally different way.

There are a few people who saw something in me that I didn't see in myself, who have invested in me in ways I could never pay back, who changed me and my life:

Mitch Beer, you took a chance on me, and then you cared enough to support what was best for me, even though it wasn't what was best for you. I'll never forget it. I'm not sure I'm wired to have a boss, but if I needed one, I'd pick you every time.

Todd Schoon, I was intimidated by you for years! I'm grateful you gave me the opportunity to know you so that intimidation could turn into admiration. Your wise advice and thoughtful support is the reason my little business turned into what it is today.

Lisa Kalmin, you changed everything. Without your stand, I wouldn't have created the relationships, wouldn't have taken the risks, and wouldn't have begun the journey of loving myself again. I'm forever grateful the universe saw fit for you to be here, at this time, so our paths could cross. Because without you, I don't know where I'd be. Thank you for caring enough to kick my ass when I need it. I love you.

And finally, Jay and JJ, again, because the best things always begin and end with you.

About the Author

Nicole's passion for eliminating gender expectations and redefining "Woman's Work" is both what keeps her up at night and what gets her up in the morning. (Well, that, and an abundant amount of coffee.)

An in-demand speaker, leadership strategist, respected coach, and host of the *This Is Woman's Work* podcast, her stalker-like obsession with confidence sets her apart from the constant stream of experts telling us to *be* confident. She actually tells how to build it, and gives actionable tools—not just stories—to *become* confident.

A fugitive of the C-suite at a Fortune 100 company, Nicole has coached hundreds of women in business, which has given her insight as to what—structurally, systemically, and socially—is and isn't serving women and leaders within an organization.

Maintaining some semblance of sanity in her different roles of wife, mother, and business owner successfully is an ongoing challenge. In whatever free time she has, Nicole enjoys reading and wine-guzzling, is an avid cheese enthusiast, a hotel snob, and a reluctant Peloton rider.